# OVERVIEW

## Overview
### Tact and Diplomacy

Have you ever said or done anything at work you later regretted? Maybe it caused embarrassment or loss of respect. Perhaps it even directly affected your job. Don't worry, you aren't the first person who's done this. But there are people who always seem to communicate with diplomacy and tact. What are the secrets to their success?

People who communicate with tact and diplomacy show sensitivity and respect to others. But that's not all. They also understand that each and every situation is different. The message has to be packaged according to who's receiving it and where the interaction takes place.

This course details the characteristics of tact and diplomacy so you may apply them in any situation. You'll learn how to communicate effectively with people by considering their communication style preferences. You'll explore how to do this in specific professional relationships with superiors, subordinates, coworkers, and customers. Once you've figured out the right thing to say, you'll also learn about the right places to say it.

Sorin Dumitrascu

## Strategies for Communicating with Tact and Diplomacy

With tact and diplomacy, workplace relationships are nurtured and can develop into meaningful connections. Unfortunately, the opposite is also true. If communication is tactless or undiplomatic, relationships suffer – or may never even get off the ground. To communicate with tact and diplomacy, you need strategies, skills, and awareness. Too often, emotional reactions and misinterpretations get in the way of tactful and diplomatic communication.

In this course, you'll learn how to communicate and develop relationships with tact and diplomacy. You'll also be given the opportunity to apply specific guidelines in a realistic scenario.

In order to develop and nurture professional relationships, you first need to build trust and rapport. Building trust is about integrity and honesty, while building rapport means finding common ground with another person. An effective way to build trust and rapport is to communicate with tact and diplomacy.

Tact comes down to recognizing the sensitivity in a situation and ensuring that whatever you say is appropriate. It enables you to assert yourself, without offending anyone.

Diplomacy comes down to being "political" or "politically correct." It requires, for example, that you take account of an organization's corporate culture when communicating.

Even though tact and diplomacy are two distinct aspects of communicating, you need to bring both together to communicate effectively.

This course will introduce you to techniques that will help you to navigate conversations in a way that's sensitive and respectful. It will demonstrate proper timing and delivery when communicating. This will enable you to deliver messages tactfully and diplomatically, without sacrificing your reputation or professional relationships.

**Delivering a Difficult Message with Diplomacy and Tact**

How many times have you been stressed or concerned about delivering a message in the workplace? There will inevitably be difficult conversations in the workplace – either with your supervisor, a colleague, or subordinate – that you'll want to avoid. This may cause you to procrastinate or avoid issues.

Delivering a difficult message with diplomacy and tact will help prevent conflict and avoid hurting the other person's feelings. This, in turn, helps reduce any anxiety you may be feeling about delivering the difficult message.

There are two main types of difficult messages in the workplace. The first involves giving bad news and the second involves requesting a change in behavior of another person. Regardless of the context, it's best to carefully plan its delivery. You should prepare the key message in advance and practice the delivery of the message.

This course explores the skills needed to help you effectively plan and deliver your difficult messages. You'll be introduced to some essential tools and techniques to draw upon when in a difficult situation. You'll also be given guidelines, which you can refer to when faced with a difficult situation at work. By following these guidelines, you'll be better equipped to manage any negative emotional reactions to your message. Finally, you'll have an opportunity to practice your new skills.

# CHAPTER ONE

*The Impact of Situation and Style*

**Tact and diplomacy**

Have you ever been left asking yourself over and over why you said what you did? Sometimes it's difficult to know exactly what to say without causing offense. Being tactful and diplomatic may seem to come easily to others, but using these tactics can require a bit of effort. Once they're practiced, though, good communication can become natural.

In business, simply doing a good job is often not enough. People are expected to participate in positive relationships within their workplaces.

Being a better communicator can help you build or improve working relationships. By displaying tact and diplomacy, you can make connections, garner respect, and command influence. You can get your message across more effectively because people will be more willing to listen.

Wendy, a manager at a bank, has an important meeting. She's missing a file promised to her by an employee, Opal. Follow along as Wendy asks Opal for the late file.

*Wendy:* Where's the file you were supposed to give me yesterday? Wendy is sharp and demanding.

*Opal:* I had a bit of trouble with it, so I asked Frank to help. I wanted to make sure it was perfect this time. I have it on my desktop; I'll send it over right now.

Opal is timid and apologetic.

*Wendy:* You're kidding, right? I gave you an easy one this time! My four-year- old daughter could do better! Plus, Frank helped? I'm not sure which one of you is less competent. Really, you're useless – both of you. Just give me the file.

Wendy is loud, mean, and full of blame.

*Opal:* I've just sent it. It should be in your e-mail.

Opal is both quieted and a bit frightened of her manager's verbal attack.

*Wendy:* This better be good. If not, there's an opening in my kid's preschool class.

Wendy is smug.

*Opal:* You're being overdramatic about this. Everyone can hear. It's really embarrassing.

Opal is unsure of herself and embarrassed.

### Reflect

What do you think of the way Wendy asked Opal for the late file?

Write down your response or enter it in a text file in your word-processor application (or in a text editor such as Notepad) and save it to your hard drive for later viewing and for comparison with the alternate opinion that follows.

## Wendy's communication approach

As you may have noted, Wendy was entitled to have the file on time. However, the way she asked for it was pushy, rude, and impolite. She could have delivered her message in a much more tactful and diplomatic way. This kind of communication is generally not tolerated in the workplace.

You may have good intentions, but your words may not always reflect this. That's why it's important to choose your reactions with care. The best way to "package" your message is to "wrap" it with tact and diplomacy. The receiver gets the same message, but takes note of the effort you put into it.

Tact is the ability to recognize and react appropriately to delicate situations. Being tactful means acting with sensitivity and respect.

While tact requires a certain amount of thoughtfulness, it doesn't come at the expense of assertiveness. Sometimes assertiveness is incorrectly thought to be the same as aggressiveness.

Being assertive means having the ability to communicate with confidence, but in a respectful way. On the other hand, being aggressive means getting what you want, no matter who gets hurt.

You can be assertive and tactful at the same time. In fact, it's probably difficult to be assertive without demonstrating tact.

If you're not considering others, you could be acting more aggressively than you think. Using assertiveness and tact together can help you get your point across without yelling or being insensitive.

That way, you'll invite others to listen to you, rather than dread what you'll say.

**Question**

Remember the conversation between Wendy and Opal regarding the late file? When Opal failed to deliver it on time, Wendy's response was both untactful and undiplomatic.

What would have been a more tactful and diplomatic response when Wendy found the late file was finally ready?

**Options:**

1. "Don't worry Opal. It's great that you asked for Frank's help. This deadline wasn't realistic. I'm sorry I put you under pressure. Can you e-mail me what you've got and I'll work with it?"

2. "It's hard to meet deadlines, but that's what we have to do – it's what's expected. Anyway, it's ready now. Please e-mail me the file right away. Thanks."

3. "I assumed it was ready, but perhaps it wasn't as straightforward as I expected. We'll talk about the problems with this file after my meeting. In the meantime, could you e-mail it to me?"

4. "If you have problems with assignments in the future, please let me know right away. That way I can make sure you're getting the help you need and that I'm getting the file on time."

**Answer:**

Option 1: This option is incorrect. Being tactful doesn't mean being apologetic. When communicating with tact, you should be sensitive, while keeping the integrity of the message you want to communicate. That's why you should be assertive.

Option 2: This option is incorrect. Wendy doesn't recognize the delicacy of the situation. Opal was trying to do a good job, but Wendy doesn't give her credit for this. Wendy comes across as being aggressive rather than assertive.

Option 3: This option is correct. Wendy recognizes the problem and the delicacy of the situation. She also remains assertive to get what she wants.

Option 4: This option is correct. Wendy is letting Opal know that she'll support her if there are any issues at work. She's showing respect for Opal while still being assertive.

**Sensitivity and respect**

Diplomacy and tact share a number of similar characteristics. The two most important are sensitivity and respect. This is true in any situation.

**Question**

Roger has been promoted to supervisor. He has to tell a former coworker, Emily, that she's performing a task incorrectly.

Which statements could Roger use to diplomatically address Emily's issue?

**Options:**

1. "I've done this job in the past. It's not that difficult. You're smart; you should be able to do it right."

2. "I've done this job in the past, so I can understand your confusion. I think I've made the same mistake myself."

3. "You've done such a good job up to this point. I'm surprised that you can't get something so small right the first time. Please fix it immediately."

4. "You've done such a good job here. This is just a small problem, but it should be fixed right away. I'm sure it won't be a problem for you, considering your past accomplishments."

**Answer:**

Option 1: This option is incorrect. This response is undiplomatic. Roger makes a weak attempt to connect to Emily. What he's missing is respect and sensitivity for her. When a compliment is given, it's backhanded.

Option 2: This option is correct. Roger uses diplomacy by trying to relate Emily's experience to his own. He's sensitive to her mistake and presents himself well. He respects her efforts.

Option 3: This option is incorrect. The message starts off with a promising connection, but then Roger adds "up to this point" and diplomacy disappears. He also notes that he's "surprised" that Emily missed the problem. He's not respecting Emily, nor is he being sensitive to her.

Option 4: This option is correct. Roger first points out what Emily is doing right, which shows he appreciates her work. Then he follows up with a bit of assertiveness about fixing the problem, but he's in no way disrespectful. He ends by connecting with Emily, by telling her that he recognizes her good work.

Being sensitive at work doesn't mean you have to be everyone's confidant. You also don't need to avoid talking about what needs to be done. You just need to recognize that the people you're dealing with are human too.

For example, say a coworker's work performance is off one day. You don't need to take the coworker out for lunch or do the coworker's work. Just keep in mind that people have bad days. You could let the person know that you recognize this and encourage trying again.

Respecting people doesn't mean that you have to like them. You just have to regard them as professionals.

For example, you may not like your manager's new policy on staff breaks. You may not even like your manager. However, you can still have respect for this person in this role. Maybe you can respect that your manager delivers the news assertively.

Sensitive and respectful people typically display three attributes in their communication approaches: good manners, thoughtfulness, and confidentiality.

See each attribute of sensitive and respectful communication to learn more about it.

**Good manners**

Having good manners isn't just about saying "please" and "thank you" – although that can be appropriate. It's about showing you're a positive part of your workplace. You can do this by being polite and following workplace etiquette.

Work is not the place to gossip. There are some subjects that should be avoided in this kind of environment. Discussing certain nonwork-related things such as sports or family can help you build connections. However, topics like politics, religion, or salaries can cause unnecessary friction.

You also should avoid talking too much or too loudly, and cutting in on or cutting off other people's conversations. If you do, sometimes a simple apology can go a long way.

**Thoughtfulness**

Someone who is thoughtful considers others. This can involve asking people's opinions. Even if you don't agree with their opinions, you get new perspectives. What's really thoughtful is hearing what they have to say. There's a difference between listening to others and just waiting for your turn to speak.

Say your coworker gives you a suggestion on how to improve your assignment, but you immediately recognize that her idea won't work. Instead of mentally preparing how you're going to respond, hear her out. She may think of something new. If not, this is an opportunity for good manners to come into play.

### Confidentiality

Confidentiality in the workplace is extremely important. If someone shares something of a discreet nature with you, it likely means that person trusts you. The information may or may not be work-related. Still, it's important to be sensitive and respectful by keeping things to yourself.

For example, a coworker confides in you that she's expecting a baby. This isn't something that's appropriate to share without her permission. Or say your manager tells you about a project that has yet to be announced. Maintaining confidentiality is not only appropriate, but may be essential to retaining your job.

Sensitivity and respect are the main ingredients of tactful and diplomatic communication. You should approach any situation with this in mind.

### Question

Which examples show tact and diplomacy?

### Options:

1. You're talking informally with a subordinate. You tell him that a friend and coworker needs to be careful because the friend is in danger of being fired.

2. A subordinate has been having personal issues that are affecting her work. You provide her with information on counseling services. However, you tell her she's still expected to do her job unless she feels she needs some time off to deal with her problems.

3. There have always been awkward silences between you and a coworker. To better connect with him, you ask what he thinks about your manager.

4. Your manager has asked that you not make personal calls at work. It's extremely important that you make just one more. You explain to your manager why this particular call is urgent and required.

**Answer:**

Option 1: This option is incorrect. This is a matter of confidentiality with the person who's in danger of being fired. It shouldn't be brought up in a conversation with another person.

Option 2: This option is correct. You're being sensitive to the person by suggesting she get help. You're also politely reminding her of work expectations. This is not being aggressive, but rather being assertive.

Option 3: This option is incorrect. While it's important to make a connection, there are some topics not appropriate for work. It's good manners to keep conversation light and not to gossip.

Option 4: This option is correct. You show respect for your manager by asking if you can make one final call. It's tactful and diplomatic to ask for permission if the call is truly important.

Good intentions and hard work are commendable. However, in the workplace, it's also essential that you use tact and diplomacy. Tact and diplomacy don't compromise assertiveness. In fact, these elements can help you build stronger working relationships. When this is accomplished, you're more likely to get what you want.

For tact and diplomacy to work, sensitivity and respect toward others are required. This includes having good manners, being thoughtful, and maintaining confidentiality.

**Identifying communication styles**

To communicate with tact and diplomacy, you need to be sensitive and respectful. However, this can be more challenging than it first seems. People are sensitive to different things. And what one person sees as a lack of respect may not be an issue for another. For example, some people think it's respectful to make eye contact, while others do not.

It's important to take into account the communication styles of others. These communication styles are based upon their preferred behaviors. There are a range of behaviors that fall within people's communication styles. This includes not only what they say, but also what they do.

For example, people may be talkative and keen to answer and ask questions. Their voices may sound enthusiastic and they might make a lot of movements with their hands. You may also notice that they'll often suggest you meet or speak on the phone rather than sending e-mails.

Other people may be shy and keep to themselves. Their voices may be soft and they may avoid attention. You may also notice that they'll say only what's necessary and e-mail instead of speaking directly to others.

Situational factors also affect communication styles. Someone who's excited will act differently than someone who's angry. And a person might be more serious when speaking to a manager than when talking to a coworker. It's all relative.

**Question**

What are some of the things that influence a person's communication style?

**Options:**

1. Who is being addressed
2. How the person is feeling
3. What the person says
4. How the person acts
5. What the person is wearing
6. What language is spoken

**Answer:**

Option 1: This option is correct. People may change their communication styles based on who they're addressing. For example, they may communicate the same message differently to a customer and a coworker.

Option 2: This option is correct. People's communication styles can change based on whether they're happy or sad, angry or bored.

Option 3: This option is correct. What people say – or don't say – is telling of their communication style.

Option 4: This option is correct. People indicate their communication styles through nonverbal behavior. These behaviors can be subtle like a dart of the eye, or very apparent like a pointing finger. Nonverbal behavior can also be picked up in a person's tone of voice.

Option 5: This option is incorrect. Communication styles are indicated by verbal and nonverbal behavior.

Option 6: This option is incorrect. While culture may influence communication styles, language is neutral.

Leroy and Stan are coworkers. Their project has gone over budget. They have to tell their manager this, and also ask for more money. Follow along as they discuss how to approach their manager.

*Leroy:* I say we go and tell her right now. I'll tell her. Leroy is direct, but positive. He's looking at Stan.

*Stan:* But how do we tell her we're already over budget by more than 50%? And then ask for more money?

Stan is skeptical.

*Leroy:* We just say it. It's already been spent. We need to continue. That's it.

Leroy is calming and convincing.

*Stan:* Well...I think we should preface it with some accomplishments of the project. What do you think? Like how it's already saved the company nearly $2 million.

Stan is genuine.

*Leroy:* She knows that.

Leroy is agreeable.

*Stan:* Yes, but maybe you can remind her? If you do all the talking, I'll back it up with the numbers. I think she'll appreciate that.

Stan is asking a favor.

*Leroy:* Yes, I can see that. We can bring the documents in too. I have no problem with that. I'll set up a meeting with her for this afternoon.

Leroy is agreeable.

Leroy and Stan exhibit different verbal and nonverbal behaviors.

Leroy wants to come right out and tell their manager about the issue. He's volunteered himself to do the talking. He thinks that what's done is done and it's time to move on. This is apparent not only by what he says, but how he says it. It's indicated in the tone of his voice.

Stan also thinks it's important their manager knows about what's going on. However, he wants to consider how she should be told. He may be a little shy. This is indicated in his words and his demeanor. He also prefers that his coworker does most of the talking. Still, he offers to do his part by bringing background information to the meeting.

You can deduce people's communication style preferences by their verbal and nonverbal behaviors. Communication styles tend to be open or closed and direct or indirect.

See each communication style preference to learn more about it.

**Open**

People who are open tend to be extroverts – that is, they're willing to share their emotions and interact more readily with others. They're energized by this kind of communication.

For example, a new coworker may come up and make introductions to team members without provocation.

**Closed**

People who are closed tend to be introverts. They prefer to keep their emotions to themselves. They also tend to interact less with others than extroverts.

For example, a coworker may only e-mail you with short requests instead of engaging in conversation.

### Direct

People who are direct tend to get right to the point. They're usually assertive. They often make decisions and handle confrontation quickly and decisively.

For example, a manager may not bother with small talk when meeting with you. Instead, the manager may prefer to say what needs to be said and move on.

### Indirect

People who are indirect tend to be less forward than those who are direct. They weigh all options before making decisions. They're also not entirely comfortable with confrontation and may shy away from it.

For example, a coworker may disagree with you, but not tell you directly, or at all.

When they talked about the meeting with their manager, Leroy and Stan's verbal and nonverbal behaviors suggested different communication style preferences.

In their conversation, Leroy was direct. He got to the point with Stan and wanted to do the same with their manager. He was also open. He's the one who started the conversation with Stan. And he volunteered to talk to their manager about the situation.

On the other hand, Stan was indirect and closed. He wanted to consider all the options before telling their manager the news. He also suggested that Leroy do the talking.

Keep in mind that communication styles are based on a number of factors. It can be easy to identify with one communication style. You may think, "That sounds exactly like me!" You may notice how people at work tend to fall into one category or another too. However, people shouldn't be categorically defined based on what they say or what they do.

The benefit of identifying preferred communication styles is having more tactful and diplomatic interactions. You'll get a general idea of how people prefer to give and receive information. From there, you can respond to their communication styles.

Antonio is meeting with his manager, Cindy, to discuss project ideas. Follow along with their conversation and consider their different communication styles.

*Antonio:* It's great that we're finally able to meet face-to-face to talk about the project. I have so many ideas, you wouldn't believe it! I tend to be a real "idea" person. Or at least that's what everyone tells me. Antonio is excited. He's directly facing Cindy and smiling.

*Cindy:* Great. Let's hear them. Cindy is only vaguely interested. She doesn't look up from her computer.

*Antonio:* Well, where to start? Really, that's the question! I was thinking that since increasing sales is one of our targets, I'd start there. Or if you'd rather, I can speak more to our efficiency situation. Antonio rambles on. He's trying to catch Cindy's attention. He uses his hands to gesture.

*Cindy:* In our e-mails, we decided to focus on sales. Cindy is abrupt. She looks at her watch.

*Antonio:* Okay, well, I have a few options drawn up in these documents. I think they're all viable solutions.

Maybe you can take some time to read them over to let me know what you think? Then we can meet again to discuss the best option?

Antonio is insulted by Cindy at first, but recovers his composure quickly. He offers Cindy files to look at.

*Cindy:* Look, I don't have a lot of time. Could you just quickly explain which you think is the best? Cindy is a bit irritated and exhausted. She looks as though she's waiting for a quick response.

*Antonio:* Well, they're all great options! You're not giving them a chance. You're not giving me a chance. Antonio is upset.

**Question**

Based on the discussion between Antonio and Cindy, which statement best describes Cindy's preferred communication style?

**Options:**

1. Cindy's tone shows how pressed for time she is in her job. Despite this, she looks Antonio directly in the eye and explains the situation to him. She's using indirect language and displays an open communication style in this conversation.

2. Cindy's tone shows she's really not happy with Antonio taking up so much of her time. This is also apparent in her body language – she doesn't even look up from her computer when he talks. She's using direct language and displays a closed communication style in this conversation.

3. Cindy's tone shows she's excited about Antonio's ideas, but has no time at that moment. Her body language indicates she's ready to listen to Antonio, but he's going

too slowly. She's using direct language and displays an open communication style in this conversation.

**Answer:**

Option 1: This option is incorrect. It's true that Cindy's time pressures can be heard in her voice, and that she tells Antonio she's in a hurry. However, she says so directly. In addition, her dialog with Antonio is short and curt. She doesn't say anything more than what's required – this suggests she tends to be closed.

Option 2: This is the correct option. Cindy sounds irritated when Antonio provides options and details. She gives him several physical indicators of this: not looking up from her computer, checking her watch, and looking impatient. When she does speak, she says only what's needed and gets directly to the point.

Option 3: This option is incorrect. Cindy's tone indicates she's slightly irritated by Antonio. Her body language shows she's more interested in finishing her work and getting to her next meeting. She gets to the point when she speaks and doesn't open herself up to Antonio.

**Responding to communication styles**

People all have their own communication style preferences. You may tend to be open or closed or direct or indirect. However, you're not limited by these tendencies. You don't need to use the same communication approach in all situations. In fact, you shouldn't. Being tactful and diplomatic means you're willing to adjust what you say and how you say it.

You have a repertoire of communication styles to choose from.

Communication styles are like clothes. You may feel more comfortable in one style than another. Maybe you like to wear casual clothes. Or perhaps you prefer suits. That doesn't necessarily mean your wardrobe doesn't include other outfits. You pick what you're going to wear based on the situation. For example, you'd probably wear a suit to meet with a bank manager to get an important loan.

The same is true for communication styles. Say you're someone who loves to discuss details. It could be appropriate to have an in-depth conversation with a coworker who feels the same way. But it may not be tactful and diplomatic to do so with a manager who's more direct.

Tactful and diplomatic communication requires you to draw on qualities from different communication styles. When speaking to someone, consider that person's communication style preferences. Is the person open or closed? Is the person direct or indirect? After you have an idea, tailor your message. Such an approach is sensitive and respectful to the person's preferences. It can also help you say the best thing, and build better relationships.

When adjusting your communication style, you may have to adjust the levels of certain qualities. These include dominance, sociability, compliance, and patience.

See each quality to learn more about it.

**Dominance**

Dominance refers to the amount of control within a conversation or relationship. People with higher levels of dominance want to be in control. People with lower levels of dominance are more passive and tend to avoid confrontation.

### Sociability

Sociability has to do with people skills. Those who enjoy interacting openly and often with others have higher levels of sociability. Those who are more reserved and introverted have lower levels of sociability.

### Compliance

Compliance deals with the ability to follow rules. People who follow rules to the letter have higher levels of compliance than those who don't necessarily do what they're told.

### Patience

Patience is the ability to endure difficult circumstances. People with higher levels of patience can persist in difficult situations without irritation. People with lower levels of patience don't have as much tolerance.

Say you're a direct person and dominance is the main quality that characterizes your communication style. However, you have to tell some very outgoing employees they have to work over the weekend. You should aim to be less dominant and more sociable to deliver your message with diplomacy and tact.

You could say something like, "Folks, I know you may have great plans for the weekend, but we really need to finish the project before Monday. We'll have to put in a few hours on it this weekend. Let's try to work out a schedule that will suit us."

You may have spoken more directly to other people in other circumstances, but by adjusting your style you've been more tactful in this delicate situation.

Adjustments in communication approaches may also be necessary when dealing with open or closed people – for example, if you have to introduce two new employees to your team.

If one of the new employees is an open person, you could let that person do a self-introduction, or introduce the person in a team meeting. You could also allow the person to make a quick speech. These kinds of things are likely to be energizing for someone who's open.

If the other employee is a closed person, you could introduce this person to team members individually. Or you could send out an e-mail with the announcement. A person who's closed is a little more shy and appreciates not being the center of attention.

Remember Leroy and Stan? They discussed how they should deliver news to their manager about going over budget. Leroy's communication style was open and direct. Stan tended to be more closed and indirect. They each wanted to deliver the information in the styles most comfortable to them. However, they should have considered the way their manager likes to do business. Because she tends to be closed and direct, elements of both their styles are needed.

They may have first tried approaching her via e-mail. This is a tactic that a person who's more closed may prefer. In the e-mail, the issue could be stated directly, but not unpleasantly. They could also ask to meet with her.

During the meeting, Leroy could speak directly, but adjust his style to be more compliant and less dominant. Stan could back up the message with some figures. He'd have to keep it straight to the point to match his manager's style.

Earlier you followed along with a discussion between Antonio and Cindy. Now you're going to be asked a second question based on the same conversation. Feel free to review the dialog if you'd like. The question immediately follows.

*Antonio:* It's great that we're finally able to meet face-to-face to talk about the project. I have so many ideas, you wouldn't believe it! I tend to be a real "idea" person. Or at least that's what everyone tells me.

Antonio is excited. He is directly facing Cindy.

*Cindy:* Great. Let's hear them.

Cindy is only vaguely interested. She doesn't look up from her computer.

*Antonio:* Well, where to start? Really, that's the question! I was thinking that since increasing sales is one of our targets, I'd start there. Or if you'd rather, I can speak more to our efficiency situation.

Antonio rambles on. He is trying to catch Cindy's attention. He uses his hands to gesture.

*Cindy:* In our e-mails, we decided to focus on sales. Cindy is abrupt. She looks at her watch.

*Antonio:* Okay, well, I have a few options drawn up in these documents. I think they're all viable solutions. Maybe you can take some time to read them over to let me know what you think? Then we can meet again to discuss the best option?

Antonio is insulted by Cindy at first, but recovers his composure quickly. Antonio offers Cindy files to look at.

*Cindy:* Look, I don't have a lot of time. Could you just quickly explain which you think is the best?

Cindy is a bit irritated and a bit exhausted. She looks as though she's waiting for a quick response.

*Antonio:* Well, they're all great options! You're not giving them a chance. You're not giving me a chance.

Antonio is upset.

**Question**

How could Antonio have adjusted his communication style to Cindy's in order to communicate with more tact and diplomacy?

**Options:**

1. He could have approached her with a higher level of sociability

2. He could have been more direct in his point

3. He could have complied with the e-mail request to focus on sales

4. He could have given her more of a chance to talk

5. He could have provided her with more detail about both sales and efficiency

**Answer:**

Option 1: This option is incorrect. Cindy is closed and direct. People who prefer these styles of communication usually shy away from talking too much and like to get to the point.

Option 2: This option is correct. Cindy is closed. She'd probably appreciate it if Antonio adjusted to her preferred style.

Option 3: This option is correct. Cindy directly wrote in an e-mail that Antonio should focus on sales. Still, he ignored the request and presented too much information.

Option 4: This option is incorrect. Cindy is closed and direct. In their conversation, she said what she needed to. In fact, Antonio should have talked less to adjust to her preferred style.

Option 5: This option is incorrect. Cindy only requested that Antonio provide information on sales. Even then, she directly asked for less detail than what he offered. His response was neither tactful nor diplomatic.

There are many factors that determine what people say or do. However, people usually tend toward one communication style or another. They can be open or closed, or direct or indirect. That doesn't mean they can't change to suit the situation.

People can alter their preferred communication styles temporarily to display tact and diplomacy. This is done out of sensitivity and respect for others. It could include adjusting levels of dominance, sociability, compliance, and patience.

## *Learning aid* - Communication Style Preferences

You can better communicate with others if you observe and take note of their preferred communication style preferences. This table outlines the four communication style preferences: open or closed, and direct or indirect.

| | Communication style description |
|---|---|
| Open | People who are open tend to be extroverts – that is, they're willing to share their emotions and interact more readily with others. They're energized by this kind of communication. |
| Closed | People who are closed tend to be introverts. They prefer to keep their emotions to themselves. They also tend to interact less with others than people who are open. |
| Direct | People who are direct tend to get right to the point. They're usually assertive. They often make decisions and handle confrontation quickly and decisively. |
| Indirect | People who are indirect tend to be less forward than those who are direct. They weigh all options before making decisions. They're also not entirely comfortable with confrontation and may shy away from it. |

## Relationship

Being tactful means being able to recognize and deal with delicate situations. The delicacy of a situation will depend on the person you're addressing, as well as where the communication is taking place. The key is to always show sensitivity and respect to the other person.

There are four main categories of people you may have professional relationships with – superiors, subordinates, coworkers, and customers. Each requires a different approach for communicating with tact and diplomacy.

Superiors can have hectic schedules. Time limitations may require you to use a more direct communication style with them. This doesn't have to come at the expense of pleasantries though.

Say Sally wants to talk to her busy manager about new project ideas. She could send her manager a meeting request via e-mail that outlines her objectives. When they do meet, Sally might only have 30 minutes to get her points across. She may have to be more direct in her communication style to do this.

She might start the meeting with a friendly greeting and some brief, but genuine, pleasantries. Then she could preface her directness by saying something like, "I know our time is limited today, so I'll get to the point."

Superiors may also sometimes want to talk to subordinates about their own problems. Superiors may have to make unpopular decisions as part of their jobs, but it's important for subordinates to be sensitive to their superiors.

**Question**

Hannah has scheduled a meeting with her busy manager. It's important she get her information across, but she only has 30 minutes to make her point. Her manager has spent the first 5 minutes talking about sports.

What could Hannah say to focus the conversation on work, while being both tactful and diplomatic?

**Options:**

1. "We should catch a game sometime after work. Speaking of work..."

2. "I'm going to be direct: I need to cut you off. I only have 30 minutes to talk to you."

3. "I like that team too. That being said, you should be focusing on work instead of sports."

4. "I like that team too. What do you think about their new player?"

**Answer:**

Option 1: This is the correct option. Hannah is sensitive to the fact that her manager wants to have a casual chat. She also creates a transition to talking about work that's both pleasant and direct.

Option 2: This option is incorrect. While Hannah is being direct, she's not being sensitive or respectful. Cutting someone off doesn't show good manners.

Option 3: This option is incorrect. Hannah starts off well. She tries to connect with her manager. However, her second sentence seems to undermine the manager.

Option 4: This option is incorrect. Hannah isn't focusing the conversation on work. If she doesn't, her message may not be heard.

When communicating with subordinates, there are a few things you can do to ensure you're tactful and diplomatic. They include staying calm and professional, providing clear expectations, showing appreciation, and giving criticism privately.

See each approach to communicating tactfully and diplomatically with a subordinate to learn more about it.

**Staying calm and professional**

When communicating with subordinates, consider how they may interpret your attitude as a reflection on their performance.

For example, Scott has had a difficult day and it isn't even noon. When a subordinate asks him for feedback on a project, he loses his temper with her. The result is that his employee thinks she's done something wrong when she hasn't.

This incident could have been avoided. Scott should have separated his negative feelings about his bad morning from his work interactions. Even if his employee had done something wrong, staying calm would have been his best option.

**Providing clear expectations**

When communicating with subordinates, it's important you provide clear expectations for them. For instance, one of Sue's employees hasn't been following the work dress code. Sue has sent her a few e-mails with helpful tips for being more professional. However, she's never come right out and told the employee that she has to change the way she dresses.

Sue should remind her subordinate about the dress code. In a private conversation, she might say, "I want to bring the company's dress code to your attention." Then she could explain exactly what it means to the employee: "You should wear closed-toe shoes instead of sandals." Finally, she could end the conversation by checking for understanding: "Do you have any questions about the dress code?"

**Showing appreciation**

Employees who feel appreciated tend to work better. You can show appreciation when communicating with subordinates to build rapport and trust. Doing so also demonstrates sensitivity and respect for their contributions.

Consider two different managers. One acknowledges employee effort. Her voice expresses genuine happiness when she congratulates her subordinates on jobs well done. She also pats people on the back to show her support. The other manager rarely shows appreciation. He thinks subordinates shouldn't be thanked for doing their jobs. Most people would rather work for the manager who shows appreciation.

**Giving criticism privately**

As a manager, it's sometimes necessary to provide criticism. For instance, Max's employees work on a fast-paced production line. Recently, one usually fast employee has started lagging behind, and it has affected output. Max addresses the issue on the floor, in front of everyone. He does so to make an example of the employee. A few days later, Max is surprised to learn the employee has quit. He also notices that the other employees are avoiding him.

It's important to provide criticism in private. When you take an employee aside to explain an issue, you respect that person's dignity. As Max learned, there are consequences to embarrassing employees in front of their peers.

**Question**

Tyson is a supervisor at a call center. A representative has been ending calls incorrectly.

How could Tyson deal with the issue so he's both tactful and diplomatic?

**Options:**

1. He could show his appreciation of a job well done in front of the employee's peers. Then he could meet with her later in a private setting to reveal what she's doing wrong.

2. He could discuss the issue at the employee's work station. Then he could show her how to correctly end her next call.

3. He could avoid talking directly about the issue. Instead, he should focus on how much he appreciates what the employee is doing right.

4. He could ask to discuss the issue with the employee privately. He should be direct and check for understanding.

**Answer:**

Option 1: This option is incorrect. While it's good to show appreciation, it should be genuine. It's also appropriate to discuss the mistake in private.

Option 2: This option is incorrect. Criticism should be given privately. There's a chance here for embarrassment. It also would've been better if he'd role-played a call ending with her.

Option 3: This option is incorrect. It's always good practice to show an employee appreciation. However, in doing so, Tyson is avoiding the issue at hand. He needs to respect his employee enough to let her know what needs to be done.

Option 4: This is the correct option. By pulling the employee aside, Tyson is showing respect – not only for her dignity, but also for her ability to do her job. Being direct doesn't mean being mean. It just means being clear and concise.

When communicating with coworkers, you can be informal and still be professional. In fact, tasteful humor can help you make connections. A good way to ensure a conversation is appropriate is to consider if you'd say the same thing if the entire workplace could hear.

For example, Kelly and Tina are friends. They're also coworkers. Outside of work, they tease each other about their personal lives. When they're in the office, they still laugh and have a good time. However, they never talk about things at work that they'd be uncomfortable sharing with others.

Tactful and diplomatic conversation also usually involves supporting team members and working collaboratively with them. Working against a coworker or providing unsolicited advice shows insensitivity.

For example, Justin disagrees with a coworker's method on a project. The way his coworker is completing the work isn't wrong – it's just different. Instead of supporting his coworker, Justin provides unsolicited advice: "You're not going be successful doing it that way."

What he should have done was show his support for his colleague's efforts by saying something like, "We have two different methods, but they both work."

**Question**

Omar's coworker has just lost a major client for their company.

How could Omar respond tactfully and diplomatically to this delicate issue?

**Options:**

1. "I'm glad it didn't happen to me. He was our best client."

2. "I told you that you shouldn't have pushed him on that deal."

3. "Look on the bright side – you don't have to deal with his bad temper anymore!"

4. "You put a lot of energy into that client. Your dedication will pay off soon."

**Answer:**

Option 1: This option is incorrect. The language Omar uses here is informal, but it's not professional. He's being insensitive.

Option 2: This option is incorrect. Omar undermines his coworker's decision. This shows disrespect for his coworker's ability to do his job.

Option 3: This option is incorrect. Omar tries to use humor to make his coworker feel better. However, it's in bad taste.

Option 4: This is the correct option. Omar's language is informal, but still professional. At the same time, he shows support for his coworker and respects him in his professional role.

Tact and diplomacy are also essential when interacting with customers. Consider Craig, who's a salesperson. Recently he received a call from an irate customer. She claimed he knowingly sold her a faulty product. Craig was hurt by this accusation. Before the customer could explain the issue further, Craig's emotions got the better of him. He responded, "The product isn't the problem. You're the problem!" He later regretted saying it, and the customer ended up hanging up on him and calling his manager.

It's easy to get defensive and aggressive when a customer is critical of a product or service.

However, it's important to listen carefully before responding and to demonstrate professionalism by not taking the issue personally. You should ask pointed questions. Then, you should try to focus on only the issues that the customer has brought up.

If Craig had let the customer finish, the outcome could have been different. Before he cut her off, the customer was going to detail her problem. If she'd had the chance to do that, Craig could have identified that she was using the product incorrectly and avoided his outburst.

**Question**

Carol is a travel agent who's trying to find the perfect vacation for a customer. When she tells him the cost of one particular trip, he insists it's overpriced and that she's not giving him what he wants.

What could Carol say to respond both tactfully and diplomatically?

**Options:**

1. "I guarantee it's the lowest price. Anything less is unreasonable. Now, can we start over?"

2. "Yes, the trip is pricey, but it's the best deal you'll get in town. Tell me exactly what you're looking for and we'll try again."

3. "I'm trying very hard to give you what you want. You're not being specific enough. I'm guessing here."

4. "Yes, the vacation is expensive. What did you expect? If you think you can get a better deal or service, you're welcome to try another travel company."

**Answer:**

Option 1: This option is incorrect. Carol is getting defensive and aggressive here. She's even managed to insult the customer by insinuating that he's unreasonable.

Option 2: This is the correct option. Carol addresses the issue directly and professionally. She then asks the customer a leading question so that she can refocus on listening to his needs.

Option 3: This option is incorrect. Carol is taking the customer's demands personally. While she asks for more specific information, the way she's asking for it isn't very sensitive.

Option 4: This option is incorrect. Carol is overreacting to the problem and getting aggressive. She needs to focus on the customer's needs.

Each professional relationship requires a different communication approach. This is especially true in difficult situations where tact and diplomacy are needed.

No matter who you're addressing, it's always best practice to treat others with sensitivity and respect. If you do this, you'll most likely get the same in return.

### *Learning aid* - Tips for Professional Relationships

You may communicate with a number of people in your workplace every day. Each professional relationship requires a different approach to ensure tact and diplomacy.

| Superiors | Consider time limitations |
|---|---|
| | Balance a more direct communication approach with pleasantries |
| | Listen and be receptive to your superior's problems |
| | Don't undermine your superior's decisions |
| Subordinates | Stay calm and professional |
| | Provide clear expectations |
| | Show your appreciation |
| | Give criticism privately |
| Coworkers | Be informal, but professional |
| | Don't say anything you wouldn't want the entire workplace to hear |
| | Use tasteful humor to make connections |
| | Support coworkers and collaborate with them |
| | Don't undermine your coworkers' decisions or give unsolicited advice |
| Customers | Listen to concerns |
| | Be professional and don't take the issue personally |
| | Ask pointed questions |
| | Only respond to the issues |
| | Don't be defensive or aggressive in your response |

## Environment

The environment where communication takes place should also be considered to ensure diplomacy and tact. Awareness of physical context helps ensure you're saying the right things in the right place.

There are a number of professional environments where you could find yourself. These include meetings with customers, team meetings, and business lunches and celebrations.

A good rule to follow no matter where you are is to conduct yourself with class. In any work environment, you're representing not only yourself, but also your organization.

Say you're having a lunch meeting with a client. Although you're physically away from the workplace, you're still conducting business. That means maintaining a level of professionalism while enjoying a more relaxed setting.

For example, your table manners may be a reflection on you. Saying "please pass the salt" is more tactful and diplomatic than reaching across the table to get it.

**Reflect**

What do you think are some of the ways that you can conduct yourself with class in any environment?

Write down your response or enter it in a text file in your word-processor application (or in a text editor such as Notepad) and save it to your hard drive for later viewing and for comparison with the alternate opinion that follows.

**Conducting yourself with class**

You may have noted that conducting yourself with class involves having good manners, using appropriate language, and dressing for the situation.

When delivering a message, it's also important to evaluate how and where the conversation should take place to avoid embarrassing the other person. There are a few questions you can ask yourself to do this:

- Can the conversation be overheard by coworkers?
- Will the person be comfortable if a customer hears the communication?
- Will the person be comfortable if the communication is in public?

Consider an example of failure to use discretion when delivering a message.

Edith has been persuaded by her coworkers to attend their company's annual awards gala. Edith is quite shy outside of work, so she's out of her comfort zone. She's utterly embarrassed when she gets a surprise award for her contributions. She refuses to go on stage.

This situation could have been avoided. Edith's coworkers knew about her shyness in public. Perhaps they could have presented her with the honor in the workplace. Or they could have told her ahead of time that she'd get the award at the ceremony. That would have given her time to prepare herself.

**Question**

Which behaviors are tactful and diplomatic?

**Options:**

1. Checking if coworkers can overhear you discussing everyday business with someone

2. Excusing yourself after sneezing during a business lunch meeting

3. Ensuring a coworker's accomplishments aren't addressed in a public setting

4. Asking a coworker in private if she'd mind doing a presentation for the team

**Answer:**

Option 1: This option is incorrect. If the communication isn't delicate, there's no need to keep it private.

Option 2: This option is correct. While sneezing can be viewed as impolite, it sometimes can't be helped. A simple "excuse me" goes a long way.

Option 3: This option is incorrect. A coworker may not mind getting accolades in public. All you have to do is ask.

Option 4: This option is correct. Asking about your coworker's comfort level with speaking in public is sensitive and respectful.

It would be nice if there was just one right way to react to every delicate situation. However, this isn't the case.

Every situation is unique, so context is essential when communicating with tact and diplomacy.

The first thing to consider is who you're communicating with. There are best practices for dealing with people at work according to your professional relationships. Superiors, subordinates, coworkers, and customers will appreciate communication approaches geared to them.

You'll also want to consider the effect the environment can have on your communication. Not only is saying the right things important, but saying them in the right place is key. Both have to be in place to ensure tact and diplomacy.

### *Learning aid* - Adjusting Your Communication Style at Work

To use this tool, fill in the communication style for the professional relationship of the person you'll address. Then, based on this information, come up with a way you could adjust to this communication style.

In your workplace, you may be involved in several professional relationships. There are preferred communication styles to use with superiors, subordinates, coworkers, and customers. After you consider the preferred communication style to use with each person, you should then decide on an approach for the specific situation. This will also take into account the context and the environment.

Sorin Dumitrascu

| | Communication style | Approach to use |
|---|---|---|
| Superior | | |
| Subordinate | | |
| Coworker | | |
| Customer | | |

# CHAPTER TWO

*Strategies for Communicating with Tact and Diplomacy*

## The benefits of tact and diplomacy

As in your personal life, relationships are a critical part of your professional life. You're likely to have relationships with coworkers, superiors, subordinates, and, perhaps, clients or customers, too. But a good relationship doesn't just happen automatically – you need to develop it. There are two fundamental components to developing a professional relationship: building trust and building rapport.

Building trust means developing a reputation for being honest and having integrity. This won't happen from words or talk alone – it needs to be backed up with action. It means you should keep promises, meet deadlines, and admit it when you make mistakes. Most of all, never do anything that will affect your reputation as an honest person. For example, if you don't know the answer to something, say so – even if you should know.

Building rapport means finding common ground with someone else. Rapport exists when two people communicate and bond on an unconscious level. When there's rapport, the relationship is cooperative and harmonious. Rapport is essential for truly effective communication, and you develop it by matching the other person's communication style. This makes the other person more open to engaging with you. For example, you could use the same words the other person uses.

**Reflect**

What do you think are ways you could build trust and rapport among your colleagues?

Write down your response or enter it in a text file in your word-processor application (or in a text editor such as Notepad) and save it to your hard drive for later viewing.

You perhaps identified that communicating with colleagues in a tactful and diplomatic manner as one way to build trust and rapport.

Tact is essentially recognizing the delicacy of a situation and saying the most appropriate thing.

Diplomacy is respecting people and their roles, and speaking to them in a respectful and pleasant manner. In doing this, you make a connection.

People who communicate in a tactless, undiplomatic way often come across as defensive or untrustworthy. Clearly, this isn't the way to foster trust. The opposite is also true in that a diplomatic and tactful approach will generate trust. Diplomacy and tact will also build rapport – creating more positive relationships, presenting you as someone of true character, and earning you the respect of others.

Communicating with tact and diplomacy helps you to communicate truthfully – but without harming your credibility or professional relationships. Being open and truthful creates trust. To communicate with tact and diplomacy, it may be necessary to adjust your communication style. Doing this builds rapport, as it shows others that you respect them and their perspectives.

Often, people's communication styles show them to be arrogant and condescending. For example, if someone comes to you with a problem, avoid giving your advice too early. Jumping in too soon with unasked-for advice gives the impression you believe you have superior intellect and greater experience. Even if this is true, it's a tactless and undiplomatic message to be communicating. Hold off with your advice, and instead listen and empathize.

It's not always easy to empathize – especially if you can't personally relate to the situation or if, in truth, it strikes you as being insignificant. However, empathy is a powerful tool. This is especially true in the workplace as corporate cultures don't generally encourage emotional displays. Empathizing with others in the workplace – showing them that it's fine to show their emotions, that you understand, and are sensitive to their problem – is the best way to build rapport.

Consider, for example, the case of Gretchen, the manager of a busy department within a government agency. Lately, Gretchen is unhappy with the work of one employee, Henry. Although she knows Henry is under pressure, particularly toward each month's end, she feels he could do better.

On approaching Henry, Gretchen acknowledges the demands placed on him. She also expresses her appreciation for his efforts at these times. She explains that, because she knows he's a hard–working and capable employee, she doesn't understand how his performance has declined so much.

Henry agrees that his standards have dropped. He says he's "burned out" from the pressure he's under at the end of each month, claiming this affects his overall performance. Gretchen expresses understanding, and promises to arrange assistance during Henry's busy periods. Henry is grateful for Gretchen's understanding, and pleased about the promise of assistance – especially as he knows that Gretchen keeps promises.

Gretchen's tactful and diplomatic approach creates trust and rapport between herself and Henry. Henry knows that Gretchen respects him, values his efforts, and understands the pressure he's under. Even though Gretchen is criticizing his work, her acknowledgement of this pressure creates rapport. They're now able to have an open and honest discussion.

Henry also appreciates the honesty and directness of Gretchen's communication. She makes her point with clarity and cohesion, ensuring that the message is understood. Gretchen's commitment to keeping promises is a big factor in the trust her staff members have in her.

The tactful and diplomatic way that Gretchen communicates contributes to the trust and rapport that exists within her department. This creates strong working relationships and a positive work environment.

### Question

What are the benefits of being able to communicate with diplomacy and tact?

### Options:

1. You contribute to positive working relationships with colleagues, superiors, subordinates, and customers

2. You create and foster trust between you and those you deal with on a daily basis

3. You aid your career progression by raising your professional profile

4. You help foster a positive environment within the workplace

5. You enhance your personal popularity among colleagues

**Answer:**

Option 1: This is a correct option. One of the reasons for communicating with tact and diplomacy is to develop and strengthen your professional relationships.

Option 2: This is a correct option. Developing rapport and trust is an important part of developing good relationships. Communicating with diplomacy and tact is a good way of building trust and rapport.

Option 3: This is an incorrect option. The point of communicating with tact and diplomacy is not self-advancement.

Option 4: This is a correct option. Communicating with tact and diplomacy helps build trust and rapport between coworkers, and strengthens relationships. This contributes to a more positive work environment.

Option 5: This is an incorrect option. The aim of communicating with tact and diplomacy is not to make yourself more popular. Even when being diplomatic and tactful, you may still be critical.

In order to develop and nurture professional relationships, you first need to build trust and rapport.

Building trust entails developing a reputation for having integrity and being honest. Building rapport entails identifying common ground with another person. This common ground could be in terms of thought, behavior, or energy level.

One of the best ways to build trust and rapport with others is to communicate using tact and diplomacy.

## Being tactful toward others

Have you ever said something embarrassing or tactless to someone? If you were lucky, you were able to laugh it off. However, sometimes these communication mishaps can make an already delicate situation worse. Such situations can usually be avoided by employing tact. Tact is recognizing the sensitivity in a situation and making sure that your comment is appropriate. It's also the ability to be assertive without being offensive.

Audio is an important component of this topic, so your comprehension will be aided by having the audio option switched on.

When resolving to be more tactful, bear in mind these principles: assess the best time to initiate a communication, listen effectively, think before responding, plan what you're going to say, and be conscious of your tone.

One part of tactfulness is assessing when it's the right time to initiate a communication. Although no time is perfect, some are better than others. Two things to consider are events in the other person's day and the physical setting.

See each component of assessing the right time to find out more about it.

### Events in the other person's day

Tact entails considering events in the other person's day. This comes down to judging whether it's a good time to have an engaging conversation.

Make sure that you're not catching people off guard or when they're under pressure. Although it's not always possible to prearrange a meeting, be sensitive to others' schedules. The best time is when nobody is rushed.

### Physical setting

Tact requires an appropriate physical setting. Certain conversations shouldn't be in public places or when others are present. When discussing a sensitive issue, privacy is essential.

Sometimes, it's best to fix a time and place so that both parties can prepare and reflect in advance. This shows respect for the other person.

Consider, for example, Alvin, the manager of an industrial supplies company. Alvin gets a complaint from an important customer, who says that a sales representative, Floyd, has been neglecting him.

Alvin can't believe Floyd would be so unprofessional. He goes straight to Floyd's office and finds Floyd in a meeting with the sales team. He loudly announces that the meeting is over, and tells Floyd he wants to speak with him immediately.

While Alvin's annoyance is perhaps understandable, his approach isn't tactful. He hasn't considered whether it's a good time for a discussion. Instead, he's catching Floyd off guard. He's also being insensitive to his schedule, and has humiliated him in front of his colleagues.

Another part of tactfulness is to listen effectively. To do this, you can follow three guidelines. First, develop awareness about the other person. Second, don't compete with the other person in the conversation. And finally, if you ask a question, be sensitive to the answers.

See each guideline to learn more about it.

**Develop awareness**

Communicating with tact requires you to develop an awareness of the other person. Listening helps you understand the other person's point of view. Listening to another's responses indicates whether that person understands your position. It also gives insight into the other person's sensitivity toward issues, willingness to discuss, and openness to your views.

**Don't compete**

Tactful communication is about conversation between people, not competitions with winners and losers. The aim shouldn't be to demonstrate superior knowledge or verbal abilities, to identify flaws in another's position, or to argue over small details. Conversations should be a mutual exchange of information, ideas, opinions, and feelings. If you communicate with a noncompetitive, nonaggressive, and more casual conversational style, others are more likely to listen, even if they disagree with you.

**Be sensitive to answers**

In addition to asking questions, effective listening means being sensitive to the answers. An effective questioning approach is to begin with broad, open questions and to actively listen to the answers. You then further develop the other person's responses by posing narrower, more focused questions. With this technique, you're using your questioning and listening abilities to explore the other person's expectations, requirements, problems, and interests.

Remember Alvin and Floyd? Alvin has angrily interrupted Floyd's meeting and demanded his immediate attention. Without waiting for the others to leave, Alvin recounts the details of the complaint.

He then accuses Floyd of jeopardizing the relationship with the customer and suggests that he may be a liability to the company.

Again, Alvin has failed to be tactful. A tactful approach would have been to ask some broad, general questions of Floyd to get his version of events. Also, Alvin has forgotten that tactful communication requires nonaggressive and noncompetitive conversation. He should also have waited for the others to leave before speaking with Floyd.

It's also important to think before responding. Sometimes you might be tempted to blurt out whatever comes to mind – and you've probably done this at some point. If so, you're aware of how it affects your credibility. In thinking about what you're going to say, you should empathize with the other person and consider the outcome you want from the communication. You should also aim to be clear, complete, and courteous in your communication.

See each recommendation to learn more about it.

**Empathize**

Before responding, you should empathize with the other person. Listening to what the other person says –

including reactions to your comments – will help you understand what this person is thinking. Often, tactless remarks stem from a failure to empathize.

**Consider the outcome**

You should decide on the desired outcome – what it is that you want to achieve. Your communication approach should be geared toward this desired outcome. Being tactful will make the other person far more willing to engage and consider your message, making it more likely you'll succeed.

**Be clear, complete, and courteous**

The message you're communicating should be clear, complete, and courteous. Keeping the number of messages to a minimum helps with clarity. And don't expect the other person to guess at your meaning. The communication must also be complete. A communication with gaps or innuendos leads to misunderstanding. Finally, your communication must be courteous – friendly, open, and honest.

Recall again how Alvin is communicating with Floyd. After confronting Floyd, Alvin turns to leave. At last, Floyd has a chance to speak. He says, "Alvin, please allow me to explain." Alvin reacts furiously, telling Floyd that there's nothing to explain, as he knows exactly what happened.

Once again, Alvin has failed to be tactful. Floyd's effort to explain was rejected by Alvin. Instead of thinking before responding, he continued with the same tactless approach. Also, his message was far from courteous.

**Question**

Which of these situations represent tactful communication?

**Options:**

1. Aware that Anita is under pressure, Larry postpones discussing her lack of punctuality

2. Dissatisfied with Ernie's work, Natalie asks open-ended questions to see if he's unhappy with his role

3. Lila doesn't respond when Mark – who is always late – comments sarcastically when she's late

4. Taking advantage of a chance encounter in the elevator, Brett calmly tells Hannah that her work is poor

5. Having been understanding many times recently, Laura becomes enraged when Manuel doesn't complete his work

**Answer:**

Option 1: This is a correct option. Good timing is a part of tactfulness. It's difficult to communicate when the other person is stressed.

Option 2: This is a correct option. Asking questions and listening to the answers is a tactful way to explore someone's concerns.

Option 3: This is a correct option. Tactful communication requires you to think before responding.

Option 4: This is an incorrect option. It's tactless to catch someone off guard with a serious issue and in an inappropriate place, such as an elevator.

Option 5: This is an incorrect option. Responding angrily is tactless.

x

## Learning aid - Developing the Right Tone

There are a number of steps you can take to develop the right tone for tactful communication.

# Communicating with Diplomacy and Tact

| Steps | Techniques |
|---|---|
| Focus on your tone and inflection | The tone of your voice should be calm, friendly, and confident. Although whether your voice is high or low is personal to you and can't be changed, it is possible to control the degree to which your voice fluctuates in line with changes in your emotional state. Avoiding dramatic fluctuations gives a sense of stability and dependability. At the same time, keeping too tight control over your voice produces a tedious monotone, which will bore listeners. |
| Find someone to imitate | To identify the tone quality that best matches your personality and your area of business, it's a good idea to find someone to imitate. Simply identify someone with the tone quality you think appropriate and copy it. This could be a TV or radio personality. Every voice has distinct characteristics, and people tend to stereotype others into categories according to these characteristics. If you want to be perceived as businesslike and professional, you need to eliminate any unprofessional or un-businesslike characteristics. |
| Practice controlling the level of your voice | The level of your voice is a factor in determining whether others perceive you as knowledgeable and confident. It's a tool for engendering trust. It's not ideal to have a voice that is either too high or too low. You can address this by doing a sliding scale to exercise the range of your voice. You can also practice speaking in a lower voice -- lower pitched voices are more credible than higher pitched voices. |
| Practice with a recorder | If you're unsure as to how your voice sounds, you could use a voice recorder. Listen to the recording and ask yourself whether it suggests tact or someone who cares. You might not like what you hear. Are you surprised by how high or low your voice is? Are there a lot of pauses or fillers in your speech? Perhaps you speak too quickly, too slowly, too loudly, too quietly, or in a monotone. Do you effectively emphasize your statements or place the appropriate stress on words to indicate their importance? |

63

## Communicating with tact

To communicate tactfully, you must consider the other person's feelings. However, you must also be aware of your expectations of the communication. One way to do this is to plan what you're going to say. Being unprepared will make an already difficult situation worse. All your efforts to understand the other person must be reflected in the words used. Even in a difficult situation, a communication delivered with positive words is easier to receive.

When planning what you're going to say, there are some important guidelines. You need to demonstrate empathy; recognize the potential for misinterpretation; use polite, positive language; get rid of personal issues; and focus on the key issue.

See each guideline to learn more about it.

### Demonstrate empathy

You can demonstrate empathy by saying something to show the other person that you have listened, understand,

and care. This means making it clear that you recognize and respect the other person's position. It also means recognizing the seriousness of the situation – at least for the other person.

### Recognize potential for misinterpretation

There's always potential for misinterpretation. Everyone has a different personal reality, and this reality influences how things are interpreted. There may be a subconscious element to what you're communicating, while there will also be a nonverbal component. You can't assume that the other person has interpreted things as you intended.

### Use polite, positive language

Irrespective of the language used by the person you're communicating with, you should always use polite and positive language. It's important not to fall into the trap of justifying rudeness or negativity by saying, "I'm just being honest." It's possible to be honest and forthright, yet also polite and positive.

### Get rid of personal issues

For the communication to be constructive and cordial, get rid of any personal issues that might arise. Conversations or discussions can easily become personal when the situation is stressful. Although insensitive remarks are sometimes made, it's important to remember that they're directed at the situation, not the person.

### Focus on the key issue

It's not always easy to maintain focus on the key issue being discussed or communicated. Trivial details, irrelevant asides, and personal remarks can sidetrack the conversation, leading it away from the real issue. Don't allow this. Identify the real issue involved and maintain focus on it.

In the example involving Alvin and Floyd, Floyd's first effort to explain himself provoked another angry outburst from Alvin. Still, Floyd tries again.

Floyd assures Alvin that he understands the importance of this customer to the company and that he shares his commitment to excellent customer service. Floyd ignores Alvin's personal remarks, recognizing that these stem only from Alvin's frustration. Instead, he focuses on the specific complaints.

Unlike Alvin, Floyd reacts tactfully. He shows empathy with Alvin's concerns. He uses polite and positive language, and ignores the personal element to instead focus on the key issue. He also took the time to plan what he was going to say before reacting.

The final element in being tactful is to be conscious of your tone. Tone is essentially the way you say something – the sound or modulation of your voice. The tone used can have more impact than what's said. For instance, a stable, well-modulated, conversational tone is persuasive, but not intimidating, whereas a quiet monotone lacks conviction and won't convince others.

There are three elements to consider when trying to find the right tone. The vocal tone relates to the voice's pitch. Generally, a lower pitch is more persuasive than a higher pitch. The inflection relates to the emphasis placed on certain syllables or the highs and lows in your voice. Finally, volume is a powerful tool that should be controlled and used effectively. While some people command attention by speaking quietly, others seek to overpower through sheer loudness.

The way your words are delivered is as important as the words themselves. For example, imagine that, after you've presented an idea to your manager, he looks you in the eye and says: "I think that's a great idea." From the words alone, that's certainly positive feedback.

However, if your manager used a sarcastic tone, saying "I think that's a great idea," he may not be too impressed.

The inflection can also alter the meaning of a word. For example, the manager could say "I *think* that's a great idea." This would suggest that, while he thinks it's a great idea, he's unsure whether others will.

In fact, the same words can have many different meanings, depending on where the emphasis is placed. If the same manager said "*I* think that's a great idea," it could suggest that he's not entirely convinced. If he said "I think that's a great idea," it could mean that he sees its merits in theory, but is unsure of its practical value.

**Reflect**

Which tones do you think are appropriate for tactful conversation?

Write down your response or enter it in a text file in your word-processor application (or in a text editor such as Notepad) and save it to your hard drive for later viewing.

In considering the tones most appropriate for tactful conversation, you may have identified a calm tone. A friendly tone is also appropriate, as well as a confident tone. While it's true that your tone should reflect the circumstances of the conversation, tactful tones tend to feature these three qualities.

Again recall the example of Alvin and Floyd. Remaining calm, Floyd offers a different perspective on the version of events that has angered Alvin.

Floyd: Alvin, I can assure you that I'm very aware of the importance of this account. I've always given this customer special attention for that reason. You know how I pride myself on the level of service I give to customers. I know how important it is. And I can honestly say I've never let the company, myself, or you down in this respect.

*Alvin:* Oh yeah, you certainly did a great job this time. Alvin is sarcastic and angry.

Floyd is calm and confident, but also a little concerned.

*Floyd:* It's true that some mistakes were made, and the level of service wasn't what it should have been.

Floyd is calm and friendly, but also slightly concerned.

*Alvin:* Come on, Floyd. it just doesn't add up. Alvin is angry, hostile, and loud.

*Floyd:* I absolutely accept that standards dropped over the past while. That shouldn't have happened.

Floyd is calm, friendly, and apologetic.

*Alvin:* So how did it happen? Alvin is a little angry.

*Floyd:* Well, things got a little crazy when Kelly retired. She was very involved with this account. Then there was the problem with the phone system. And then I was out ill for five days. But I have a good relationship with Mr. Foster. I know I can sort it out. I'll call him straightaway.

Floyd is gentle, but confident.

*Alvin:* Well, I guess I can understand that. Alvin is calm.

Despite the delicacy of the situation, and Alvin's aggression, Floyd's tone is tactful and professional throughout. He uses a calm, friendly, and confident tone. His tone is also steady, well-modulated, and conversational, which contributes to his success in convincing Alvin of his position.

As a result, Floyd appears professional, credible, and tactful. This is in contrast to Alvin, who, by speaking in sarcastic and aggressive tones, comes across as tactless and unprofessional.

**Case Study: Question 1 of 2**

Follow along as Kathy, a departmental manager in a publishing company, speaks to Nancy, one of her employees, about her poor punctuality in recent weeks.

Kathy: Hi Nancy. Thanks for making time to speak with me. I know you're busy right now, and I do appreciate it. Kathy is calm, friendly, and confident.

Nancy: What's the problem? Nancy is defensive, and a little hostile.

Kathy: Well, I want to have a quiet word with you about your punctuality. I've noticed that you've been quite late for work on a number of occasions over the past few weeks. Kathy is calm, friendly, and serious.

Nancy: Kathy, if you're unhappy with the work I'm doing, just say so. But if this is just about me being five or ten minutes late every so often, well... I think you're making a big deal out of nothing. Nancy is slightly aggressive.

Kathy: No, Nancy, it's not about that – your work is terrific, as it's always been. But we're not talking about five or ten minutes, are we? It's much more than that.

You've been two hours late on some days. Kathy is encouraging and placating.

Nancy: I didn't realize you were that obsessed with time. Nancy is sarcastic.

Kathy: My concern is that your being late so often is contributing to delays on some of the projects we're working on. A lot of the others in the department rely on you for guidance and decisions. If you're not there, they can't do their jobs either. Do you understand where I'm coming from with this? Kathy is serious, but calm and friendly.

Nancy: Well, I guess I can understand that. I'll make more of an effort from now on. Nancy is mildly apologetic.

**Question:**

Which statements correctly describe the tactful tones used by Kathy?

**Options:**

1. Despite some provocation, Kathy used a calm tone throughout

2. Kathy's approach and tone were friendly

3. While remaining friendly and calm, Kathy used a confident tone

4. Kathy raised the tone of her voice to ensure Nancy knew who was in charge 5. Kathy spoke in an apologetic tone so not to aggravate Nancy

**Answer:**

Option 1: This is a correct option. Even when Nancy questioned Kathy's motives, she retained a calm tone.

Option 2: This is a correct option. Kathy began the conversation by thanking Nancy for making the time to see her.

Option 3: This is a correct option. Even when challenged by Nancy, Kathy's tone was firm and confident.

Option 4: This is an incorrect option. Kathy didn't raise the tone of her voice. A raised tone isn't appropriate in tactful communication.

Option 5: This is an incorrect option. Kathy didn't use an apologetic tone. To do so wouldn't have been tactful, as it would have been inconsistent with the message.

**Case Study: Question 2 of 2**
**Question:**
In what way could Kathy have been more tactful?
**Options:**
1. Kathy could have begun with a broad, open-ended question about Nancy's lack of punctuality
2. Kathy could have been more sensitive to the timing of the conversation and avoided catching Nancy off guard
3. Kathy shouldn't have reacted emotionally to Nancy's responses

**Answer:**
Option 1: This is the correct option. By using a questioning and listening technique, Kathy could have gained an insight into Nancy's behavior.

Option 2: This is an incorrect option. Kathy ensured tactful communication by not catching Nancy off guard.

Option 3: This is an incorrect option. Kathy's communication was tactful because she didn't react emotionally.

There are certain principles that you can follow to make sure your communication is tactful and diplomatic.

First, you should assess when it's the right time to initiate a communication. This means taking account of the physical location and events in the other person's day. You should also listen effectively, which includes asking questions to develop your understanding. And think before responding, as opposed to "blurting out" the first thing that enters your head. Another important principle is to plan what you're going to say. This includes demonstrating empathy, recognizing how your message could be misinterpreted, using polite and positive language, and focusing on the key – rather than any personal – issues. Finally, you should be careful about the tone you use.

## Learning aid - Five Guidelines for Communicating with Tact in the Workplace

There are certain guidelines that you can follow to make sure your communication is tactful and diplomatic. You should assess when it's the right time to communicate, listen effectively, think before responding, plan what you're going to say, and be conscious of your tone.

| Guidelines | Considerations |
|---|---|
| Assess when it's the right time to communicate | Events in the other person's day and the physical setting |
| Listen effectively | Ask questions and be sensitive to the answers |
| Think before responding | Empathize with the other person, consider the outcome you want from the communication, and ensure that your communication is clear, complete, and courteous |
| Plan what you're going to say | Demonstrate empathy, recognize how your message could be misinterpreted, use polite and positive language, get rid of personal issues, and focus on the key issue |
| Be careful about the tone you use | Appropriate tones include calm, friendly, and confident |

**Being aware of the corporate culture**

Have you ever wondered why it's easier to spot undiplomatic communication than it is to spot diplomatic communication? Maybe it's because diplomatic communication is simply communication as it should be. You probably like to think that your communication is always diplomatic. But is it? Being diplomatic is more than just being polite. It requires you to consider and follow some specific guidelines.

Although tact and diplomacy are two different aspects of communicating, both must be brought together to communicate effectively.

Being diplomatic requires you to be aware of your organization's corporate culture. In simple terms, this involves being "political" or "politically correct."

Tact is more about recognizing and being sensitive to the delicacy of a situation and other people.

**Reflect**

What do you think you could do to be diplomatic in the workplace?

Write down your response or enter it in a text file in your word-processor application (or in a text editor such as Notepad) and save it to your hard drive for later viewing.

You perhaps identified your general behavior and relations with colleagues as being factors in whether or not you're regarded as being diplomatic. These relate to the two general principles that should be followed to be diplomatic in the workplace – be aware of the corporate culture of the organization, and be a good coworker.

Being diplomatic requires awareness of the organization's corporate culture. There are several layers to an organization's corporate culture. Superficially, corporate culture is the way things are done in an organization. Beneath this, corporate culture is the system of informal, unwritten rules. At a deeper level are the common values that guide these rules, with fundamental assumptions being deeper still.

See each layer of corporate culture to find out more about it.

**The way things are done**

The way things are done in a particular organization includes formal structures, systems, and processes, and things like how people dress and the language used.

Generally, these things are obvious. A lot of them come from official policies and codes of conduct. These include policies or guidelines on acceptable behavior, acceptable language, or dress.

**Informal, unwritten rules**

The informal, unwritten rules within an organization give a deeper insight into corporate culture – this is the way things are really done. These rules won't be stated in any official policy, but will instead be gradually revealed to a new employee during the socialization process.

This is the organization's protocol. These rules stem from tradition and precedent, and may be completely different from formal policies or codes of conduct.

**Common values**

Every organization has a system of common values, beliefs, and understandings. This system generally determines actual behaviors, systems, and attitudes.

The common values are the source from which the informal, unwritten rules originate. Common values can include things like teamwork, a high regard for customers, and punctuality.

**Fundamental assumptions**

Fundamental assumptions are at the core – and the deepest level – of what an organization's corporate culture is all about. These assumptions are what employees believe to be fundamental and distinctive about their organization.

They tend, though, to be unspoken and assumed, rather than stated and promoted. These tacit assumptions sometimes reflect the official organizational philosophy.

For example, some organizations' corporate philosophies cherish and encourage innovators. Where this is genuine, one fundamental assumption among employees is that innovation and taking risks are central to their company.

It's important to "tap into" the corporate culture, and ensure that what you say and do are consistent with it.

Failing to adhere to the way things are done will be particularly obvious to others – and may come across as undiplomatic.

For example, take the case of a company where most people dress casually in the office. One person might choose not to dress casually because of a purely personal preference. However, it could be interpreted as an effort to stand out from others. This wouldn't be diplomatic, and may cause resentment.

Being diplomatic also requires you to follow the informal, unwritten rules of an organization. For example, there may be an unwritten rule in your company that requires you to run any idea past your coworkers before going ahead. Not doing this would be undiplomatic.

**Question**

Which of these examples show an awareness of corporate culture?

**Options:**

1. Despite being accustomed to brash communication in her previous employment, Bonnie – following the example of others – uses quieter tones in her new employment

2. Despite his own personal dislike for risk, Gregory encourages his subordinates to be innovative and take calculated risks as this is part of the company's corporate philosophy

3. Even though others routinely check with the manager before releasing any data, Juan doesn't as there's no written rule to say he should

4. Although teamwork appears to be a common value within her company, Ulrike – who works better alone – avoids getting involved in any team-based initiatives

**Answer:**
Option 1: This is a correct option. Language used and the way people communicate is a component of corporate culture. It's diplomatic to adhere to this.

Option 2: This is a correct option. The fundamental assumptions that employees have about their company – which could include an innovative nature – are an important part of corporate culture.

Option 3: This is an incorrect option. Informal, unwritten rules are a part of an organization's corporate culture. It's diplomatic to follow these rules.

Option 4: This is an incorrect option. Common values – such as teamwork – are part of an organization's corporate culture. It is undiplomatic to behave contrary to these values.

**Being a good coworker**

Being diplomatic in the workplace is also about being a good coworker. This means that you should develop an awareness of your coworkers. It also means that you give credit where due, and share blame when things go wrong. It's also important that you don't make negative comments about coworkers.

See each aspect of being a good coworker to find out more about it.

**Develop awareness of coworkers**

Developing an awareness of your coworkers is one of the easiest ways to avoid problems with them. It means making an effort to learn about the pressures they're under.

You can develop awareness simply by watching how they work – knowing what their responsibilities are, what their daily challenges are, and what their busy periods are.

It's also useful to talk to them – simply talking to people instead of speculating on their decisions or actions is the best way to get perspective.

**Give credit and share blame**

It's important to give credit to others who've contributed to any achievement or success. You should also take your share of the blame or responsibility for mistakes or failures.

Taking credit for others' achievements will cost you dearly in the long term. It'll badly affect your relationship with others, and make them less inclined to assist or cooperate with you in the future.

When speaking of successes that have been a team effort, always use "we" instead of "I" to make it clear that others were involved.

**Don't make negative comments**

Don't ever make negative comments about a coworker – or any comment that you wouldn't make directly to that person.

Never make a comment – either oral or written – when you're angry or frustrated.

If you do have to make a critical comment about someone, be sure that you know all the relevant facts before you form – and, in particular, express – your opinion.

Consider, for example, Renee and Max, account managers with an advertising agency. Before going on vacation, Renee asked Max to handle the final pitch to a potential client – a lucrative contract she'd been chasing for three months.

Even though teamwork is a central part of how the agency operates, Renee knew she was asking a lot of

Max. Still, in her absence, Max delivered the final pitch – and won the contract for the agency.

Not only will this contract double the agency's annual revenue, it will give it the opportunity to express its creativity, which is something it's especially proud of.

Follow along as Renee – who has just heard the good news – phones Max to thank and congratulate him.

*Renee:* Hi Max! I just heard the news... Congratulations! You did a great job. And thanks so much for stepping in like you did.

Renee is pleased and excited.

*Max:* Thanks, Renee. I'm glad it worked out well – and more than glad to have been able to help.

Max is pleased and appreciative.

*Renee:* Well, I really do appreciate it, Max. I know how busy you've been with your own projects – especially the two renewals. I'm sure you were under a lot of pressure.

Renee is pleased and grateful.

*Max:* No problem at all, Renee. Teamwork! That's what we're all about! I have to say, though, I can't take all the credit – Peggy and Glen played a big part. It wouldn't have happened without them, that's for sure.

Max is upbeat and enthusiastic.

*Renee:* Of course, yes. And Louise, too. Wasn't she supposed to be involved? Renee is understanding, but with a tone of trepidation.

*Max:* Well, as it turned out, Louise was a little tied up with her own project. I guess she's still getting used to her new role. She didn't feel she could spare the time. I understood that.

Max is diplomatic and conciliatory.

*Renee:* Sure. So what do you think clinched it for us in the end? Did you get any feedback?

Renee is serious but still positive.

*Max:* Definitely our creativity. I could tell the client was impressed. I think we're starting to get recognized for that. And our commitment to clients, as well. Just as you suggested, we put a lot of emphasis on both of these things during the pitch.

Max is enthusiastic.

Renee: Fantastic, Max. And congratulations again. I'll call Peggy and Glen now to congratulate and thank them, too.

Renee is upbeat and grateful.

Both Renee and Max handle their conversation diplomatically. Renee acknowledges that Max was under pressure with his own projects, which demonstrates awareness of her coworker. Max readily acknowledges the contribution made by Peggy and Glen – sharing credit. Neither Max nor Renee comment negatively about Louise. Max and Renee also embrace the common value of teamwork and commitment to clients, and the fundamental assumption that creativity is a central characteristic of their agency.

**Question**

Which of these examples suggest the individual concerned is a good coworker?

**Options:**

1. Keen to get the attention of senior management, Sam ensures that he mentions only his contribution to the success of the project

2. Having noticed a dramatic decline in Daniel's standard of work, Martha concludes that he's lost interest in his job and shouldn't be considered for promotion

3. Before asking Maura to proofread some promotional literature, Cheryl checks that she has the time to do it

4. Despite firmly believing that Jill is lazy and incompetent, Bill makes some discreet inquiries before reporting this to his manager

**Answer:**

Option 1: This is an incorrect option. An important part of being a good coworker is to give credit to others who contributed to any achievement or success.

Option 2: This is an incorrect option. A good coworker doesn't speculate on the motivations behind others' decisions or actions, but instead speaks to the person before jumping to conclusions.

Option 3: This is a correct option. Being a good coworker means having an awareness of others – which includes knowing whether a request is reasonable.

Option 4: This is a correct option. Being a good coworker means being sure that you have all relevant facts before making a critical comment about someone.

Effective communication means communicating with tact and diplomacy.

To be diplomatic in the workplace requires you to be aware of the corporate culture of the organization, and be a good coworker.

Corporate culture includes things such as the way things are done in an organization; the system of informal, unwritten rules; the common values that guide these rules; and the fundamental assumptions.

Being a good coworker involves following some basic guidelines. You need to develop an awareness of your coworkers, give credit where due, and avoid making negative comments about coworkers.

*Learning aid -* **Communicating with Diplomacy**

In order to demonstrate awareness of the corporate culture, you should be aware of the following:

- the way things are done – The way things are done includes formal structures, systems, and processes, and things such as how people dress and the language used. These tend to be obviously apparent, and often stem from official policies and codes of conduct.
- informal, unwritten rules – The informal, unwritten rules are, in some respect, the way things are really done. However, these rules won't be formally stated anywhere. Instead, they'll be gradually disclosed to a new employee during the socialization process. This is the organization's protocol.
- common values – It is generally a company's system of common values, beliefs, and understandings that determine actual behaviors,

systems, and attitudes. These values are the foundation of the informal, unwritten rules.

- fundamental assumptions – Fundamental assumptions are at the core – and the deepest level – of what an organization's corporate culture is all about. These assumptions are what employees believe to be fundamental and distinctive about their organization.

To be a good coworker, you should do the following:

- develop awareness of coworkers – This means making an effort to learn about the pressures your coworkers are under in their day-to-day jobs. This awareness can come from simply watching how they work – knowing what their responsibilities are, what their daily challenges are, and what their busy periods are.

- give credit and share blame – It's very important to share the credit for any success or achievement with everyone who made a contribution. Not doing so will severely affect your relationships with coworkers. You should also take your share of the blame or responsibility for mistakes or failures.

- don't make negative comments – You should never make a negative comment about a coworker, or even any comment that you wouldn't make directly to that coworker's face. If you must comment critically about a coworker, make sure you have all of the facts before doing so.

-

***Learning aid* - Developing an Awareness of Coworkers**

To use this tool, fill in the details of your coworkers' jobs to help you develop an awareness of them.

One of the best ways to avoid any difficulties with your coworkers is to develop an awareness of them. To do this, you should try to find out everything you can about the pressures they're under in their day-to-day roles. This can be done simply by observing them, which will give you a good insight into their responsibilities, the challenges they face, and their particularly busy periods.

When you understand your coworkers' jobs, the complexity of their tasks, and the pressures they're up against, you can better assess the difficulty of any request you might make. This makes you a better coworker.

**Communicating with tact and diplomacy**

Although there are subtle differences between tact and diplomacy, they go hand-in-hand and should be used together when communicating. A mistake in one can make the entire communication ineffective. A communication that's tactful, but not diplomatic, can have a negative effect on your relationship with the other person. The same goes for a diplomatic, but not tactful, communication.

The guidelines and principles for communicating with tact and diplomacy focus on what to do and say, what not to do and say, and some considerations when communicating with others:

- assess the best time to communicate, which means taking account of events in the other person's day and the physical setting
- listen effectively, which entails asking questions and being sensitive to the answers, and

recognizing that effective communication is about conversation rather than competition

- think before responding, which means empathizing with the other person, considering the outcome you want, and ensuring your communication is clear, courteous, and complete
- plan what you're going to say, which includes recognizing the potential for misinterpretation, using polite and positive language, and focusing on the key – rather than any personal – issue
- be conscious of your tone, recognizing that the way you say something is as important as what you say
- be aware of the corporate culture, and follow any protocol that's a part of this culture, and
- be a good coworker, which means developing an awareness of your coworkers, sharing credit, and avoiding making any negative comments

In any communication – in fact, in anything you say – polite and positive language should predominate. It's a critical aspect of tactful and diplomatic communication.

As well as exhibiting politeness, the language you use should fit with the corporate culture of your organization. Most importantly, always avoid vulgarity and offensive or inappropriate jokes or remarks.

You should now have a good understanding about the guidelines for communicating with tact and diplomacy. Over the next pages, you'll have the chance to apply your knowledge.

Consider this situation. You're attending a meeting – with every other employee at your company – in which the company's senior finance manager, Gilbert, is presenting a new efficiency plan.

As part of his presentation, Gilbert announces that the initiatives included in the plan will cut the company's costs by 30%, representing a savings of $300,000. Not surprisingly, this elicits a very positive response from those in attendance – particularly as earlier estimates suggested that savings would be closer to $100,000.

Upon hearing this, you immediately suspect this is an error. It just doesn't add up with what you expected when you looked over the figures briefly last week.

You feel slightly responsible for this. You're the manager of the company's Research Department, and it was two of your employees, Gary and Audrey, who produced the figures for the Efficiency Plan.

Although both Gary and Audrey are inexperienced employees, you thought that having them work as a team – which is standard practice in the department – would ensure against any errors.

Audrey, who is sitting beside you, leans across and quietly says, "I'm not sure about this figure. I think we should only have included current costs in the calculation, but Gary insisted it should be current and fixed costs. I tried to explain but he wouldn't listen." You suspect Audrey's right, and know you must tell Gilbert about this mistake.

**Question**

Since you decided to tell Gilbert about the mistake in calculating the cost savings of his efficiency plan, now you must decide when is the best time to deliver this news.

Which approach demonstrates good timing?

**Options:**

1. Seeing as it's essential Gilbert knows about this before proceeding any further, you stand up immediately and announce the error

2. Deciding that it's best to be discreet, you quickly write a short note and ask Gilbert's assistant to pass it to him while he's speaking

3. After he finishes his presentation, you ask to be permitted to make an announcement – in which you communicate this important information

4. You wait until you're back at your desk, and then you send Gilbert a brief e-mail outlining the error and offering to meet him to discuss it further

**Answer:**

Option 1: This is an incorrect option. It wouldn't be tactful to announce this information so publicly, nor to catch Gilbert off guard, especially when he's clearly engaged in making his presentation.

Option 2: This is an incorrect option. Communicating the message in this way would catch Gilbert off guard, which wouldn't be tactful.

Option 3: This is an incorrect option. This communication shouldn't be made publicly or when Gilbert is off guard. Moreover, this approach would likely embarrass Gilbert, which wouldn't be tactful.

Option 4: This is the correct option. Tactful communication entails considering the physical setting and the other person's schedule. This approach would be private and sensitive to Gilbert's schedule.

Diplomacy and tact aren't the same thing, and one without the other risks making your communication ineffective.

To ensure your communication is effective, you must show the listener that you've listened and understood, and that you care. It's necessary, too, to focus on the key issue, instead of any personal issues that may arise during the conversation. You should also ensure that you share credit where due – and take your share of the blame if appropriate. Finally, avoid making negative comments. And make sure you always comment with discretion.

And remember, always be careful to use polite and positive language in every communication you make.

# CHAPTER THREE

*Delivering a Difficult Message with
Diplomacy and Tact*

**Difficult messages**

How many times have you swept a problem under the carpet, only for it to come back to bite you? In the workplace, there are sometimes difficult conversations that you'd rather avoid. Consequently, you may procrastinate or avoid issues. This is counterproductive and allows negativity to fester. The best response to a difficult situation is to carefully plan your message and deliver it with diplomacy and tact.

Difficult messages in the workplace include announcing layoffs, disciplining employees, or giving constructive feedback. Even if you don't manage staff it's possible that you'll have to deliver difficult messages to peers.

There are two main types of difficult messages. The first is giving bad news. The bad news is most likely something that's beyond the sender or receiver's control. The second is requesting a change in behavior of a subordinate or colleague. When requesting a change of behavior, the sender wants to address an issue that requires the receiver's acceptance and commitment to change.

See each type of difficult message to learn more.

**Bad news**

Delivering bad news can be very difficult for anyone to do, and sometimes managers must deliver bad news on behalf of the company. For example, they might have to announce layoffs or salary cuts.

In such situations, it's best not to procrastinate about the issue. Deliver the formal communication outlined by senior management without trying to "soften the blow." Keep to the facts, and don't criticize the decision or the people who made it.

**Change in behavior**

Changing behavior is difficult . To be effective, it requires the desire to change rather than mere compliance to a set of rules. Using a collaborative approach, which respects and acknowledges the needs of both parties, encourages personal development.

Say, for example, you're giving some colleagues feedback on their abrupt communication style. Acknowledging that this isn't a reflection on their personalities, but perhaps a lack of experience, will help them be more open to your feedback. This is preferred to a directive approach – that is, telling a colleague that a behavior is "wrong."

The way you deliver a difficult message can have a greater impact on the way it is received than the actual content of the message itself. Using diplomacy and tact allows you to preserve a positive and productive relationship in spite of the difficult message you have to deliver.

**Question**

Which of these messages do you think are likely to be difficult to deliver?

**Options:**

1. Stephen, a team leader in an insurance company, has to tell his entire team that salaries will be cut by 20%

2. Sophie, a bank team leader, must ask a subordinate to change his telephone manner due to recent client complaints

3. Maria, a sales manager, tells her team members that they must reach their sales targets in order to receive a bonus

4. Peter, a store manager, must advise all employees to attend mandatory health and safety training

**Answer:**

Option 1: This option is correct. Telling people they'll be making less money is difficult, and is an example of giving bad news.

Option 2: This option is correct. Asking people to change their telephone manner is difficult, and is an example of asking for a change in behavior.

Option 3: This option is incorrect. Telling team members they must reach their targets is a standard message to all sales staff members. The message is likely to be standard company policy.

Option 4: This option is incorrect. Advising employees to attend mandatory training is a standard message. This message shouldn't be difficult to deliver as no one is singled out.

This book focuses on delivering difficult messages, and how to do that with diplomacy and tact. Though not the focus of this book, some general guidelines for communicating with diplomacy and tact in the workplace apply.

## Communicating with Diplomacy and Tact

There are two general principles that you should follow to be diplomatic in the workplace – be aware of the corporate culture of the organization, and be a good coworker.

### Be aware of corporate culture

In order to demonstrate awareness of the corporate culture, you should to be aware of several things:

- **The way things are done** includes formal structures, systems, and processes, and things such as how people dress and the language used. These tend to be obviously apparent, and often stem from official policies and codes of conduct.
- **The informal, unwritten rules** are, in some respect, the way things are really done. However, these rules won't be formally stated anywhere. Instead, they'll be gradually disclosed to a new employee during the socialization process. This is the organization's protocol.

- It is generally a company's system of **common values**, beliefs, and understandings that underlie actual behaviors, systems, and attitudes. These values are the foundation to the informal, unwritten rules.
- **Fundamental assumptions** are at the core – and the deepest level – of what an organization's corporate culture is all about. These assumptions are what employees believe to be fundamental and distinctive about their organization.

**Be a good coworker**

To be a good coworker, you should take several actions:

- **Develop awareness of coworkers**, which means making an effort to learn about the pressures your coworkers are under in their day-to-day jobs. This awareness can come from simply watching how they work – knowing what their responsibilities are, what their daily challenges are, and what their busy periods are.
- **Give credit and share blame.** It's very important to share the credit for any success or achievement with everyone who made a contribution. Not doing so will severely affect your relationships with coworkers. You should also take your share of the blame or responsibility for mistakes or failures.
- **Don't make negative comments.** You should never make a negative comment about a coworker, or even any comment that you wouldn't make directly to that coworker's face. If you must

comment critically about a coworker, make sure you have all of the facts before doing so.

Some other guidelines that you can follow to make sure your communication is tactful and diplomatic include assessing when it's the right time to communicate, listening effectively, thinking before responding, planning what you're going to say, and being careful about the tone you use. Each of these guidelines has its own considerations.

**Preparing the message**

Due to its sensitive nature, the delivery of a difficult message should be planned. Conversations can become difficult where issues are important to either party – either professionally or personally. If emotions run high, it's easy to lose focus and diverge from the facts. You may experience stress and fear of looking bad or upsetting your colleague. Good planning and preparation prior to the meeting can help overcome any fear or stress.

When planning the delivery of a difficult message, you should first prepare the message. Second, it's best to practice appropriate nonverbal behaviors. Finally, plan when and where you'll deliver it.

The first step in delivering a difficult message is preparation. Preparation requires you to carefully analyze in advance the details of what you need to communicate. Ensure your facts are correct, explore all viewpoints, and think about the possible reactions from the other person.

Your focus should be on the goal of the message and not on the person. Define clear, realistic, achievable outcomes for the meeting.

You then develop the message that you're required to deliver. To maintain credibility, be prepared to back up your statements with facts and examples, as you will likely be challenged on them.

You can apply some helpful principles when analyzing a situation. First, don't oversimplify the issues. Then separate all the relevant issues, and separate any conclusions you've made from the facts.

See each principle for analyzing the situation to learn more.

### Don't oversimplify

Because it's daunting to try and tackle several issues at once, you may inappropriately try to roll these problems up into a simplified "super-problem." For example, labeling a person as "difficult" or "a trouble-maker" isn't productive. Isolate specific issues of a person's actions or behaviors that can be addressed positively.

### Separate issues

Say you're planning to speak to a colleague about a particular issue, such as performance. It's best to avoid drawing in other issues – for example tardiness – to back up your statements. This only signals inadequate preparation.

If you come prepared to the meeting with facts and examples, you shouldn't need to draw on alternative issues. This could confuse the recipient, and make it more difficult to gain agreement on an action plan to resolve the issue at hand.

### Separate conclusions from facts

When you prepare for a difficult conversation, make sure you separate facts from conclusions. This involves challenging any assumptions you may make.

For example, a new team member has been late for work three days in a row. You conclude this is a sign that he lacks commitment and is unprofessional. However, you don't have all the facts. Perhaps he's adjusting to new personal circumstances at home, a new baby, or a sick or recently deceased relative.

Consider Maria's situation. She's a team leader in a fund management company. One of her team members, Neil, has made several significant errors on a client account, miscalculating how much money was owed to a client. This has cost the company money in compensation payments.

Maria is worried about meeting with Neil to discuss the issue. He can be argumentative and has upset people in the past. It's important Maria doesn't oversimplify the issue by labeling Neil as difficult. She must respect Neil by laying out the facts of the situation, without making any challenges to him as a person.

In this meeting, Maria must separate the issue of Neil's previous behavior and focus on the errors. His previous behavior should've been dealt with at the time, and shouldn't merge into the current issue. Furthermore, she must separate any conclusions she has made about Neil, and have an open mind to any explanation he provides.

When preparing a difficult message, the key is to develop an assertive message. That way, you will make your point clearly and articulately, and yet stay sensitive and respectful. You can therefore avoid hurting the other person's feelings. Ultimately, you want to maintain good working relationships with people.

Effective assertive communication is characterized by nonjudgment, disclosure of your feelings, and clarification of the effect of the action or behavior. You can then clarify the action or behavior you expect.

Remember Maria? In order to be assertive, she'll state the details of the error without judgment. She'll then disclose her feelings about the situation, saying, for example, "I feel under pressure to reduce the error rate." She should then clarify the facts, and finally, gain agreement for a way forward.

When the difficult message involves asking for a change in the other person's behavior, using the "I" statement approach is beneficial. This approach involves pointing out the undesirable behavior followed by the impact it has on you and, if possible, your preferred change in behavior. Examples of "I" statements are "I would like..." or "I feel that..."

Once the facts have been acknowledged, focus on the solution. When proposing a solution, use "we" statements to show support. But bear in mind, you must make sure the responsibilities of both parties are agreed.

Inappropriate statements of judgment often involve accusatory "you" statements, which can cause defensiveness and emotional upset. An example would be saying "you've made a big mistake." You shouldn't place blame on the individual or focus unnecessarily long on the problem.

**Question**

Maria, the team leader in a fund management company, is planning her conversation with one of her team members, Neil. She contemplates ways to open the conversation about Neil's error rate.

Which of the options is the most appropriate?

**Options:**

1. "Neil, your mistakes are unacceptable. You're really making life difficult for me! You need to improve your numerical accuracy immediately!"

2. "Neil, the error report notes that there are three errors this month belonging to your client. I feel under pressure to reduce errors, so I'd like us to work out an action plan for reducing your client's error rate."

3. "Neil, I'd love it if the team could reduce errors to avoid compensation payments. What do you think?"

**Answer:**

Option 1: This option is incorrect. This approach is aggressive and uses "you" statements. Maria is accusing Neil, and being overly emotional.

Option 2: This is the correct option. It's an assertive approach that doesn't judge Neil. Maria uses "I" statements and focuses on solutions to the problem.

Option 3: This option is incorrect. This is a passive approach and Maria has failed to acknowledge the facts or assert an opinion.

The wording of the message should be carefully chosen to show sensitivity and respect. It often helps to open the conversation with a positive point. However, you should avoid the trap of complimenting for the sake of being diplomatic, as this can appear condescending to the receiver. Also, be careful not to over-compliment. Being too positive may dilute the importance of the difficult message and confuse the listener.

When delivering bad news, you should follow two guidelines. First, show respect for the company choice and strategy. For example, if announcing layoffs, state the facts without editorializing or criticizing the decision or the people who made it.

Case Study: Question 1 of 2

Scenario

For your convenience, the case study is repeated with each question.

Pamela is a team leader in a bank. She's concerned about the number of recent errors by one of her team members – Bill – who has recently moved to her department. There have been several complaints from clients.

Pamela heard from Bill's previous manager that he tends to react badly to constructive feedback. Apparently, one time, Bill became combative toward a colleague.

Pamela's manager has asked her to address the issue with Bill as soon as possible. Answer the questions in order.

**Question**

Her goal is to have a calm and measured conversation with him, and to gain agreement from Bill on an action plan to improve his numerical accuracy.

Which statement best describes how these goals can be achieved?

**Options:**

1. She should highlight that Bill's performance is already questionable given his history of inappropriate behavior, and a second mark on his record is cause for concern.

2. She can accept that there may be a reasonable explanation for Bill's mistakes. Perhaps he needs more training, or isn't getting the support he needs from others. She should ask him what he needs to improve his performance.

3. To avoid having Bill become aggressive toward her, Pamela should say that the client made several complaints, and she's stuck with the unfortunate task of doing the client's dirty work.

**Answer:**

Option 1: This option is incorrect. Pamela shouldn't draw other issues into the conversation.

Option 2: This is the correct option. Pamela isn't making assumptions or judging Bill. Instead, she offers further support.

Option 3: This option is incorrect. Pamela shouldn't take a passive approach and shift the blame to the client.

**Case Study: Question 2 of 2**

Pamela is now developing the message she wants to deliver to Bill. What are the most appropriate approaches to addressing her goals in the meeting?

**Options:**

1. Pamela should acknowledge that Bill probably has a reasonable explanation. She should invite him to generally "catch up" and talk broadly about compensation payments. He should bring up the issue himself.

2. She could tell Bill she's concerned about everyone's errors, then acknowledge his specifically. She could then say that she's made no assumptions about them, and she's open to hearing his interpretation.

3. She should tell him that his lack of attention to detail is an issue she takes very seriously. She should also tell

him that his actions are affecting the team's credibility, and he should fix it immediately.

**Answer:**

Option 1: This option is incorrect. Pamela is using a passive approach. She is avoiding the issue by not addressing it directly.

Option 2: This is the correct option. Pamela is using "I" statements by telling Bill she's concerned. She states the facts, and isn't making assumptions.

Option 3: This option is incorrect. Pamela is being unnecessarily aggressive and using "you" statements. She's not focusing on a shared solution to the problem.

**Preparing delivery**

After preparing your message you need to practice delivering it. And you have to plan when and where you'll deliver it.

The actual words used in conversation play only a limited part in communication. Nonverbal behaviors are in fact more important when delivering a difficult message. Appropriate nonverbal behaviors include maintaining calmness and a professional tone. Also, keep emotions to a minimum to avoid the situation getting out of hand. Be aware of your voice levels to maintain a respectful volume. And finally, maintain eye contact in an appropriate way.

It's appropriate to role-play the pending conversation with your own manager, or HR, to get feedback on your delivery. Practice helps fine-tune your communication style, and can help you to be calmer when delivering the message. By practicing with a trusted colleague, you can release your own emotions and stress prior to the meeting.

In most cases, difficult messages will be confidential – for example, in giving bad news. It's inappropriate to discuss an individual's situation with colleagues other than your own manager and HR.

The final step in planning the delivery of a difficult message is to choose when and where you'll deliver the message.

Finding an appropriate time to have the meeting will avoid the meeting having to be cut short because of work deadlines. Make sure you allow plenty of time for the meeting.

Choose a private setting to deliver the message and give the receiver time to digest it. The receiver may become upset and need time to refocus. This will avoid potential embarrassment for the receiver in front of peers.

**Question**

What are the correct actions to take in preparing to deliver a difficult message?

**Options:**

1. Prepare the delivery by gathering facts and examples to back up your statements

2. Tell colleagues to make themselves available in case the individual needs emotional support

3. Choose a time and location convenient to the receiver of the message

4. Practice talking to make sure your voice is at an appropriate level, and your tone is calm and professional

5. As you will find the situation difficult, find the first available opportunity that suits you

**Answer:**

Option 1: This option is correct. This is a good preparation method for any challenges to your message.

Option 2: This option is incorrect. Difficult messages should be given privately. It's inappropriate to share with others.

Option 3: This option is correct. The receiver will need time to deal with the difficult message and will be more comfortable in a familiar environment.

There are two main types of difficult messages in the workplace, and they involve giving bad news, or requesting a change in behavior of a subordinate or colleague. When approaching the delivery of a difficult message, you should first prepare the message. This involves focusing on the message and not on the person. Also, back up the message with facts and examples.

The message you develop should be assertive to ensure you'll make your point clearly and articulately, and yet stay sensitive and respectful to the receiver. Second, it's best to practice appropriate nonverbal behaviors to keep emotions to a minimum and to adopt a calm and professional tone. Finally, plan when and where you'll deliver the message.

# *Learning aid* - Nonverbal Behaviors

| Nonverbal behaviors | Guidelines for using the behavior |
|---|---|
| Calmness | If you're well prepared for an emotional reaction, you're more likely to remain calm. When the unexpected happens, and emotions run high, it's easy to "lose your cool." |
| Professional tone | A professional tone conveys assertiveness and confidence in the message. Also, a level, well-modulated conversational tone is persuasive without being intimidating. Remember, being overly empathetic may come across as condescending. |
| Emotions kept to a minimum | Being "emotionally intelligent" is the ability to identify, understand, and manage moods and feelings, in both ourselves and other people. It's important to be self-aware and identify moods and feelings in ourselves and understand how these affect other people. Once we're aware of our own emotions, we can manage them effectively. |
| Awareness of the voice volume | Your voice is one of your vital tools in communication. Words spoken in anger give an entirely different message than when the same words are said in a moderate volume. When emotions run high, voice volume often increases. The key is balance – not too loud, but not whispering either. |
| Maintaining eye contact | The eyes are an important part of nonverbal communication. Those who stare off into space or keep their eyes glued to their feet do not inspire much attention or confidence. Good eye contact emphasizes a point and establishes trust. |

111

### *Learning aid* - **Preparing a Difficult Message**

To use this tool to prepare your message, you can print the table below and complete the empty rows to keep note of your planning. Alternatively, you can use a spreadsheet or word-processing application to create a table with multiple rows. Then you can complete it onscreen and also save it as a template for future reference.

When delivering a difficult message the "I" statement" approach is beneficial. This approach involves stating a factual behavior followed by the impact it has on you, and if possible your preferred change in behavior. Examples of "I" statements are "I would like..." or "I feel that..." Planning these ahead of time will make it easier when you are actually delivering the message.

# Communicating with Diplomacy and Tact

| Steps | Notes for delivering your difficult message in the workplace |
|---|---|
| Describe your dilemma: | |
| List the facts: | |
| Goal of the meeting: | |
| Key "I" statements to make in the meeting:<br><br>1.<br><br>2.<br><br>3.<br><br>4.<br><br>5. | |

**Handling a difficult conversation**

Consider a difficult message you've previously had to deliver in the workplace. It may have been a conversation with a subordinate, a colleague, or a customer. How did you feel about delivering the message? Were you well prepared? Did you later reflect on the experience and wish you'd done it differently? Did you wish you were more tactful and diplomatic?

**Reflect**

Diplomacy and tact are essential communication skills. What do you think are the benefits of being able to deliver a difficult message with diplomacy and tact?

Write down your response or enter it in a text file in your word-processor application (or in a text editor such as Notepad) and save it to your hard drive for later viewing and for comparison with the alternate opinion that follows.

**Benefits of delivering a difficult message with diplomacy and tact**

As you may have noted, one benefit of being diplomatic and tactful with others is that you're more able to handle other people's emotions and reactions. This allows you to deliver the message in an effective and professional way that prevents conflict and avoids hurting the other person's feelings.

Another benefit of diplomacy and tact is that you can reduce any fear or anxiety you may have about delivering the difficult message.

You can follow several general principles when delivering a difficult message:
- be assertive, but not combative
- show empathy
- acknowledge the other person's feelings
- demonstrate respect
- listen effectively, and
- be aware of your tone and body language

See each principle to learn more about it.

**Be assertive**

It's easy to become aggressive during a difficult conversation. Remember, it's not about winning, but being focused on a solution to the current problem. Being assertive is about balance, and dealing with difficult reactions in a calm and measured way.

**Show empathy**

Being "emotionally intelligent" involves being able to identify, understand, and manage moods and feelings in ourselves and others. Empathy, therefore, is understanding someone else and trying to put yourself in that person's shoes.

**Acknowledging feelings**

You can demonstrate empathy by acknowledging the feelings of others, especially when they're different from your own. The key to ultimately controlling your own emotions is self-awareness. And this can help you be more understanding of others. Examine and reflect on your interactions with colleagues – both the negative and positive ones.

**Demonstrate respect**

It's always important to respect others and treat them as you'd like to be treated yourself. Also, be careful to respect boundaries and personal space. Ask questions when you're unsure.

Furthermore, try not to make assumptions or conclusions about what makes people "tick" based on their communication style. For example, just because people can be argumentative in meetings doesn't mean they're not sensitive to your words or actions.

**Listening effectively**

The benefits of listening can't be overstated. If a person feels a colleague has really heard a message, it's much more likely that the person will be receptive to finding a mutually beneficial solution to the current problem. The danger of not paying attention is that you will miss the one or two key pieces of information that will allow you to understand what makes the other person "tick."

**Tone and body language awareness**

Nonverbal cues of tone and body language account for the overwhelming majority of our communication. Using tones and body language showing confidence and openness is an effective way to build rapport.

These principles don't work in isolation; they're intertwined. Consider the principle of listening, for example. Active listening – feeding back literal or emotional content to a listener to demonstrate understanding - shows empathy, and acknowledges feelings with sensitivity and respect. Listening passively, on the other hand, is merely the perception of listening. For example, passive listening could include nodding and making listening sounds when you've actually reached conclusions before the person has finished.

Of course, you can listen well only if the other person has the opportunity to speak. Asking open-ended questions gets better results than asking closed-ended questions – questions with few choices, such as a yes or no answer. Another way to improve your listening skills is to summarize and paraphrase what the other person has said. Examples are "So you're saying that..." or "If I understand correctly then..." or "Let me get this straight...."

Now consider the principle of being assertive. This helps you avoid a combative situation. When difficult conversations fall apart, it's often because at least one person has a combat mentality. This type of mentality strives to identify a winner and a loser, instead of a winning situation.

An assertive person listens actively, letting the other person finish the sentences. Being assertive also means acknowledging the other person's point of view. When the other person is finished, an assertive person paraphrases to summarize the other person's point of view. For example, "I understand that you need..."

When people become overly aggressive, assertiveness becomes combativeness. This results in people using passive listening, being impatient, and interrupting or talking over the other person. They then often use expressions such as, "But listen to me, what I'm saying is..."

**Question**

Say, for example, a customer service agent is in a position where a refund can't be given to a client due to a settlement period that has just expired. The client has asked if he can explain his situation, and why he missed the deadline.

Which would be the best way to handle the conversation?

**Options:**

1. "There's no point. As I've said already, the contract has a very clear end date written on it. There is nothing I can do about it."

2. "Please do. I'll make notes. I need to have a very clear understanding of the situation to determine if we can find a solution in the framework of our company policy."

**Answer:**

The customer service agent is talking over the customer. He's not using active listening skills.

Empathy and acknowledgement of other's feelings are important when delivering a difficult message. Empathy can go a long way to avoiding a combative situation. Once you're aware of your own emotions and the emotions of others, you can manage them effectively toward finding a solution.

The skill of building empathy and rapport involves active listening, reading emotional cues, asking questions, demonstrating sensitivity, and making good eye contact.

There are, however, misconceptions about empathy. Being empathetic shouldn't be considered a passive approach. That is, showing empathy isn't about agreeing with someone, it's about understanding and showing respect for that person's opinions. You shouldn't become emotional, especially if the receiver is angry or upset.

Consider the following situation. Harriet is a team leader in a media company. She must give some bad news to Polly, a member of her team. Polly is going to be laid off. Follow along as Harriet delivers the difficult message.

*Harriet:* Hi, Polly. Thanks for meeting with me today. As you're aware, the company is in financial difficulty and has economized as much as possible. Unfortunately, the decision has been made to reduce staff. You're going to be laid off, as of today.

Harriet is calm.

*Polly:* Oh no! What am I going to do? I've been working here for ten years! My husband can't support me and our kids alone! Why me? Can't you do anything?

Polly is upset.

*Harriet:* Listen, Polly, it's not my fault! I'm scared for my own job too. It's the senior managers – they're only thinking of profits for shareholders. They don't care about us.

Harriet is flustered.

**Question**

Which statements correctly describe how Harriet delivered the message and handled the reaction from Polly?

**Options:**

1. Harriet correctly showed empathy for Polly when she acknowledged she's worried about her own job, and she may end up in the same situation.

2. Harriet started the conversation in a professional way, but reacted to Polly inappropriately by mirroring negative emotions.

3. Harriet didn't demonstrate active listening skills, since she didn't answer Polly's questions or address her concerns.

4. Harriet's delivery of the message was too aggressive. She should've softened the blow for Polly. She did however recover by acknowledging Polly's feelings.

**Answer:**

Option 1: This option is incorrect. Polly became emotionally upset and fearful, and Harriet reacted to that negative emotion. She shouldn't have become emotional, especially since Polly was upset.

Option 2: This option is correct. Harriet reacted emotionally to Polly. She shouldn't have allowed herself to become emotional, especially since Polly was upset.

Option 3: This option is correct. Harriet should've listened to Polly and addressed Polly's concerns about why she'd been identified for the layoff.

Option 4: This option is incorrect. Harriet delivered the facts in a calm and professional manner. However, she didn't acknowledge Polly's feelings, and instead reacted badly to her negative emotions.

The importance of tone of voice was evident in the conversation between Harriet and Polly. Harriet started with a calm and professional tone. Her voice level was appropriate – not too loud or too quiet.

However, Harriet didn't manage to maintain the appropriate tone throughout the conversation. She became emotional. Her voice level and her pitch raised as she became upset. She therefore lost her ability to continue delivering her message with tact.

Remember, keeping your tone calm and professional, and controlling your voice level, is crucial when delivering a difficult message.

**Reflect**

How do you think Harriet should have handled Polly's reaction?

Write down your response or enter it in a text file in your word-processor application (or in a text editor such as Notepad) and save it to your hard drive for later viewing and for comparison with the alternate opinion that follows.

**Handling a difficult conversation**

You may have thought that Harriet should've shown empathy. Polly expressed her fear and the difficulty of her situation. Harriet should've listened and acknowledged Polly's feelings by saying, for example, "I'm sorry. You must feel awful." And she should have said it without becoming emotional herself.

While these principles apply to delivering a difficult message in any situation, sometimes the context of the relationship you have with the other person can have an effect on your message. You may want to alter your message depending on the relationship. For example, if you're a subordinate speaking to a supervisor, or if you're talking to a coworker or colleague, or to a client or customer.

See each relationship to learn more.

**Supervisor/subordinate**

If delivering a difficult message to a supervisor – for example not being able to meet a previously agreed-upon deadline – it's best to demonstrate sensitivity to the situation and think about how it impacts the supervisor. Try to be very clear and make your supervisor aware of a difficulty as soon as possible.

**Coworker or colleague**

If delivering a difficult message to a peer, a more collaborative approach is best. The use of the "I" statement is effective in this context. People are generally more likely to want to help if you share your feelings or concerns. But if you start with a "you" statement, they're more likely to become defensive.

**Customer or client**

If delivering a difficult message to a customer or client external to the organization, it's advisable to focus on needs, and apologize when necessary. You should think about the customer's possible reactions to the message and demonstrate sensitivity.

**Case Study: Question 1 of 3**
**Scenario**

For your convenience, the case study is repeated with each question.

Abu is working on project with Linda. He's finding their working relationship strained. Although he has had glowing reports from Tom, his supervisor, Linda makes derogatory remarks about his work. Follow along as Linda and Abu discuss the issue.

Abu: I understand you want to express your opinion. Working on this project can be frustrating at times, but your remarks are a problem for me. I'd like us to work out a way to give each other constructive feedback. Abu is calm.

Linda: Well, I can't help making remarks when you make silly suggestions to Tom. They never work! I don't know why he always agrees with you! Linda sounds aggressive.

Abu: Oh, I'm sorry you didn't like it Linda. I did put a lot of work into it, and Tom did like the idea... Abu speaks quietly and is apologetic.

Linda: I've been here longer than him, and I know it won't work. And, while we're giving feedback, you spend too much time pacifying the clients and I have to pick up the real work... Linda sounds aggressive.

**Question:**

Which statements correctly describe how Abu handled the reaction from Linda?

**Options:**

1. As Linda's tone was aggressive, the only way to successfully deal with her behavior is to show a similar emotion.

2. Abu's approach was appropriately noncombative. If he had been more assertive, it would've antagonized Linda further.

3. Abu correctly acknowledged Linda's feelings, and showed active listening skills by summarizing and paraphrasing her comments.

4. Abu's response to Linda's comments wasn't assertive. He was defensive and apologetic.

**Answer:**

Option 1: This option is incorrect. It's not advisable to mirror negative behavior. Abu should've acknowledged Linda's feelings and behaved in an assertive manner.

Option 2: This option is incorrect. Abu's approach was passive. It's possible to be assertive in a calm and professional way so as not to intensify negative behavior.

Option 3: This option is correct. Abu listened to Linda and acknowledged her feelings, even though he didn't agree with her point of view.

Option 4: This option is correct. Abu didn't have to apologize to Linda. His ideas were supported by their superior, and he values customer service.

**Case Study: Question 2 of 3**

Which statement correctly describes Abu's tone of voice during his conversation with Linda?

**Options:**

1. Abu's tone is too quiet and hesitant. He comes across as being passive.

2. Abu's tone was appropriate to balance Linda's aggressiveness. It was calm and professional.

3. Abu's tone was calm and professional. His voice level was right. He came across as being assertive.

**Answer:**

Option 1: This is the correct option. Abu's tone was too quiet and hesitant. A more assertive approach would've been to speak louder and more confidently.

Option 2: This option is incorrect. Although Linda was aggressive, Abu didn't use his tone to express confidence and he came across as being passive.

Option 3: This option is incorrect. Abu wasn't assertive in his conversation with Linda – he was passive and quiet.

**Case Study: Question 3 of 3**

How could Abu have handled Linda's reaction with more diplomacy and tact?

**Options:**

1. When Linda challenged his work priorities, Abu should've been more confident in his beliefs that client service is a valuable use of his time

2. When Linda challenged his work priorities, Abu should've matched her assertive tone to be heard

3. When Linda criticized his ideas, he should've demonstrated listening skills and respect by further encouraging her to fully explain her point of view

**Answer:**

Option 1: This is the correct option. An assertive approach would've been a more professional and effective solution.

Option 2: This option is incorrect. Linda's tone was aggressive, not assertive. It's only advisable to match positive voice levels and tone.

Option 3: This option is incorrect. Abu needed to be assertive and confidently stand by his work priorities.

There are several principles that you can follow to help you deliver a difficult message with diplomacy and tact. First, choose an assertive approach instead of an aggressive or passive approach. Also, use empathy and acknowledge feelings without mirroring negative emotions.

You should prioritize active listening skills, and show respect to everyone you interact with. Finally, pay attention to people's tone and body language. Use positive tones and body language, and always remain calm and professional if the other person becomes emotionally upset.

While these guidelines apply to delivering a difficult message in any situation, there are different relationship contexts within which you may have to deliver a difficult message. You may have to deliver a difficult message to a supervisor, a colleague, or perhaps a customer or client.

**Practice delivering a difficult message**

You're now going to practice delivering a difficult message in a simulated scenario. Remember the key guidelines you need to follow when delivering difficult messages in the workplace.

You've learned that it's best to focus your message on the goal – or the change of behavior – and not on the person. The goals should be clear, realistic, and achievable.

When presenting the message, don't oversimplify the issues by labeling the person in a negative way. Also, separate all the relevant issues. In addition, remember to separate any conclusions you've made from the facts.

Using the "I" statement approach is an excellent way to show sensitivity and respect when giving a difficult message.

It's also helpful in a difficult meeting to be aware of your tone and body language. Watch the body language of your listener and be considerate of the impact your message is having on him or her.

A decision to be assertive means you're more likely to make your point clearly and articulately. Listening effectively, and demonstrating respect for the other person are possibly the two most important interpersonal skills that yield positive results.

When delivering bad news beyond your control – such as announcing layoffs – you really need to show respect for the company's strategy and decisions. Also, don't spread responsibility for bad news unnecessarily. This can easily happen when someone is looking for a scapegoat to abdicate responsibility themselves.

In this topic you've reviewed the guidelines for delivering a difficult message, and practiced using those guidelines to deliver a realistic message in the workplace.

Using the guidelines for diplomacy and tact will help you deliver your message and handle the other person's reactions effectively, which will lead to a more productive outcome for all parties.

Printed in Great
Britain
by Amazon